The Manual:
A Hustler's Guide to Better Living
Through Proper Business Etiquette

By Jus One

PUBLISHING

Printed in the United States of America
First Printing, 2015
ISBN 978-0-692-52438-1
HDB Publishing LLC
PO Box 25702
Philadelphia, PA 19144
www.HdbPublishing.com
First Edition

For Alym,

"May your greatest thoughts become things."

Daddo

The Manual:
A Hustler's Guide to Better Living Through Proper Business Etiquette

By Jus One

Table of Contents

Author's Note

The contents of this book have been designed to help expand the minds of business owners and those seeking to own businesses. It is in no way intended to glorify the sale of illegal narcotics nor endorse any illegal activity. It is important for this to be very clear before proceeding into the confines of this text. This manual has been crafted carefully to show the reader how to apply various business principles to their businesses. With that being said, I truly hope this book is used to help entrepreneurs worldwide to create businesses that better their communities and create conducive environments for the children to grow and do the same.

"I been in this game for years, it made me a animal/
It's rules to this shit, I wrote me a manual/
A step by step booklet for you to get/
your game on track, not your wig pushed back"

The Notorious B.I.G.

Introduction

Okay, first things first. I think the wisest thing for me to do right now would be to take the two fifteen-thousand pound elephants out of the room and clear the air. Is this really a book about selling drugs? Well, the answer to that is quite simply yes and no. This is a book about the art of business and more importantly it's about the etiquette required to succeed in business. This is the end of the "lemonade stand" approach and the beginning of a much more realistic look at the aggressive nature of commerce. There is a rapidly growing movement of those who are ready to punch the clock one final time, to clock out and take the leap into the sea of entrepreneurship.

What many of these newfound entrepreneurs will find is that there is simply nothing that could have prepared them for what they are about to endure other than shared experience. This is by no means an attempt to deter people from attending a business school and acquiring knowledge of corporate structures. It is more of a practical approach to applying information received, rather than storing useless data that effectively amounts to nothing.

For me, the drug game was my business school where I learned invaluable lessons on what does and what doesn't work in the real world of business. I've often found that schools can handicap the brain at times, by making you feel like you know something that you couldn't possibly know without experience. There is a classic scene in the movie "The Karate Kid" where Mr. Miyagi walks in on Daniel practicing karate kicks while staring at a book. He looks at Daniel and says, "Karate..learn from book?" The look on Daniel's face is priceless, but not unique. It's the look that thousands of people in business courses share when confronted by an entrepreneur with hands on experience. With that being said, the drug game offers no course. It offers no fake sense of you passing a class and now being ready. Its reward is success, yet it is far from guaranteed. Welcome to the real world of business!

Throughout my journeys in the street I've realized that there was a clear difference between a hustler and a drug dealer. This very same difference lies between a businessman and a business owner. To be clear, I'll say the act of dealing drugs does not give you the right to be classified as a hustler, and in the same regard, owning a business does not make you a businessman. The hustler and the businessman have the ability to shape and mold their operations. They do not leave things to chance, because they are mentally engaged to the idea of their own success. This is the simple reason why some businesses fail and some succeed, and why some hustlers prosper, and drug dealers don't. This is often misconstrued with the notion that we all want money. Being mentally engaged to your success is much different from simply wanting money.

When peeling back a layer or two, you will find there are many business owners who are nothing but employees with their name on the paperwork next to the word owner. You will also find in the street on a number of corners, workers disguised as free roaming street entrepreneurs in charge of their own destiny, while the reality of the situation couldn't be further from the truth. They are not in charge and have given up control, and in some cases never established control to give up. The outcome is that they are not the boss, the business is. The business is running their lives, so they can't possibly run the business. They are being moved and shifted rather than moving and shifting. This is when the feeling of slaving for your company sets in and initiates the inevitable. The end is near.

Establishing, gaining, and keeping control, all relies on the etiquette applied to your business practices as well as the practices of others surrounding your business. In a nutshell all of the business degrees in the world won't matter without the contents of this book. They are great to have just like a life-raft but a life-raft can't save you from all the ocean has to offer!

The Second Elephant

Yes, it is now time to remove that second elephant from the room who was probably getting ready to take a shit and stink up the place even more. That second huge fifteen-thousand pound elephant has my name on it, so let's get to it. Who am I and why the hell should you listen to me? After all, we're talking about people's businesses and livelihoods. Let's be real, people's lives are at stake. What have I done that was so great, and what exactly is it that I have to offer? Well, before I answer these questions for you, allow me to frame the conversation by asking you a question first. When Michael Jordan speaks on his successes and the journey to becoming a champion, is it only valid to someone interested in becoming an NBA star? Is there nothing to learn from watching a television show such as the Sopranos, unless you are interested in becoming a rising mob boss? If you have answered these questions rationally, I will begin with my humble beginnings and what led me to being as qualified as I know I am, and I'm positive that rational minds will agree. Pay close attention and you will learn how a kid from way Uptown Philadelphia, grew several businesses in some of the most dangerous neighborhoods in the country with the use of one word, Etiquette.

Chapter One:
Drug War Veteran

The Beginning

If I start from the beginning I have to start with a childhood story, because that's when the hustle began for me. As a young child the thought of selling drugs was never an option for me. I was full of potential and ambition yet I seriously lacked focus. Nothing could hold my attention. I was constantly in search of something different and new, and at the time I had no idea that this was the case. After six grade I started to feel like school wasn't for me. This didn't mean that I wasn't going to attend. It just meant that I felt there was nothing left for me to prove. I knew that I was capable of completing the work and with the right amount of focus could become all of the things my teachers told me I could be. In my mind, after six grade I had graduated myself. The "know it all" nature of adolescence had began to take over. In my seventh grade school year I began hanging out with a group of kids that shared similar interests. The fact of the matter is, besides rap music and girls, we were interested in nothing at all. It wasn't long before the marriage between idle time and rap music introduced me to my first love, Mary Jane.

My love affair with this particular substance could be a book in itself. I think after my first time smoking I had formed a habit, one that is still with me today. Now don't get it twisted, you could buy weed in my neighborhood but it wasn't as readily available as it was in other neighborhoods. Although we could have certainly used it, my parents' pride wouldn't allow them to apply for the free lunch. Instead they opted to give me ten dollars every Monday for the two dollar a day school lunch. Little did we know, with the money I had been receiving for lunch my business had already been funded. By way of our childhood grapevine we had discovered a weed store (yes I said store), that sold ten dollar dime bags big enough to smoke three cigars as opposed to the normal two cigar bags that you could find almost anywhere. This was the moment I had been supplied. I had stumbled into the beginning. The beginning of smoking up my lunch on Monday and feeling stupid and hungry all week at lunch time that is.

It wasn't until one cold morning I showed up to school after smoking, reeking of my true love's scent, that I had an accident in my first period class that caused word to spread like wild fire. I was sitting at my desk and burped out a cloud of weed smoke that must have been somehow trapped in my lungs. It wasn't able to grab the teacher's attention but it seemed that every kid had heard what happened by the end of the day. Later that day I was in class when I heard a whisper from the kid next to me who I barely knew. "Yo you got weed?" Was he asking to buy my true love from me? No way I'm selling this! I only smoked one blunt. I've got two left. I could see that he wasn't going to let up and finally gave in and sold him the remaining weed, which actually was a normal size dime bag. As I walked down the hallway after class with my high wearing off it started to settle in. I just got high for free today, and I still have lunch money. By now I'm sure you can tell I am no rocket scientist, just someone moving with a natural progression.

One day while frequenting our favorite weed store which was actually a Jamaican owned convenience store that conveniently sold the biggest dime bags I'd ever seen, I learned a series of things that were pivotal in the shaping of how I would conduct myself in every business setting from then on. Five of us packed in a car, this time all looking to purchase. It had given us an advantage that I didn't see coming. I was elected to go in and make the purchase of five dimes. I slid fifty dollars under the plexiglass window and out came six dimes. It was now time for a split second decision. There was no way I was going to tell the store, but I was torn between sharing the good fortune with the entire car or capitalizing off of the small gain. I chose to operate fairly and got back in the car and excitedly said, "They gave us six". To my surprise, there was no surprise. "They do that all the time. If you buy enough, they give you one". This made way for four very different yet valuable lessons that I will go into great detail explaining later in this book.

Lessons from the story

Lesson One:
Morality

The first lesson from this scenario was morality, and everything begins from here. Business in itself is based on a mixture of both the truth and lies. Knowing the right time for each of these things relies on your moral compass. For instance, the truth may very well be that you have a great product that will help someone to do whatever it is that they have purchased it for. Now in the case where a customer asks you where you bought it, and how much you paid for it, will surely require the stretching or caging of the truth. In these cases the lie will still serve everyone. The customer has a great product and you've received payment for it. The boundaries are crossed when the lie only serves you. Then your moral compass has been broken and will in turn stain your business's reputation. The fact of the matter is that it wasn't my reward for being the one to go into the store. It was a collective effort. The fact that there were six bags given for the price of five meant that everyone in the car had contributed to the sixth bag, and everyone should get a piece.

Now bare with me for this might seem trivial, but it is an often overlooked key component to running a business. These are the building blocks of an empire. It's the win-win situations that create longevity, and that's where success lies. For the hustlers, I'll sum it up by saying, "You think people wanna go somewhere and feel like they're getting cheated? Yea aight"

Lesson Two:
Buying in Bulk

Lesson two from this trip was simple enough, buying in bulk and knowing how to do so. I'll elaborate on that further in the chapter on consignment and the art of it, so for now we'll let sleeping dogs lie. What I will say now is this was a lesson I was able to learn quickly and swiftly at the age of fourteen due to following my moral compass and not a compass of greed.

Lesson Three:
Creative Marketing

The third lesson learned was in creative marketing. What exactly attracted us to this particular spot? What kept us coming? As I've stated, ten dollar dime bags can be purchased all throughout the city on a number of corners. For me, as a customer the experience kept getting better and better. This is when a business is alive, and living businesses have much greater odds of surviving. This will also be expounded upon deeply in the chapter on marketing.

Lesson Four:
The Partner/Customer

The fourth and final lesson of this trip is a bit complex. It's about the reaction I received after returning to the car. When I found out that buying large quantities would give me more than I had paid for, it opened a world of possibilities in my head. I was full of new ideas on how we could make this profitable for us. The one thing that would linger, is how did these guys know this and not feel the same way? The nonchalant attitudes were a problem for me, and this is the perfect example of the Partner/Customer. The truth is the only thing that made them partners in what I was strategizing, was me allowing them in on my thoughts. Other than that these friends of mine were nothing more than average customers. You should apply this to your own businesses. Ask yourself what do your partners have to offer? Do they share the same ambition as you? What ideas do they bring to the table, and do the ideas work? You should have these answers before partnering up with anyone. It will eventually save you plenty of money on migraine medicine if you do, and help you to know if you're trying to turn a glorified customer into your partner.

The Making of a Criminal

Let's fast forward. After a few lackluster attempts at selling nickel bags for a profit that almost always went up in smoke, I did an eleven month stint in a juvenile facility for "being a kid", and also being unable to keep a clean urine for the probation I had received for "being a kid". While somewhere in America children were being gifted Sweet Sixteen parties and cars for their birthdays, I was handcuffed on a bus traveling back to Pennsylvania from Texas for mine. It was during this stay that my life had taken a surprising turn. I was now officially a criminal.

I returned home at the age of sixteen and served another hellish probation and was forced into a detention school for my junior year. In this school I learned the art of observation. Kids kicked out of schools all over the place were sent to this one school to babysit them until their sentences were up. Hmmm, wonder what you would learn in a place like this? How about how to stay in trouble without getting in trouble? I managed to convince my counselor that I was fully rehabilitated while making some valuable connections along the way. I quickly realized that even in a school full of criminals I would come across more customers than hustlers, and because I had the fortitude to go and get it, even the hustlers were customers, prompting me to learn the value of the connect!

One day in school during lunch, out of the clear blue I was hit with "You sell weed right? How much for a quarter pound?" Now maybe it was the excitement of jumping to another level, or the look in his eyes that said, "This guy can't pull it off" that fueled my fire, but needless to say I had a new project on my hands! "Let me see what I can do. I'll let you know something tomorrow". When I left school that day I felt employed. No time to hang out, I was on a mission. It wasn't exactly a good feeling I must admit. I was overwhelmed with the pressure of not being able to deliver. I felt that if I couldn't deliver, then I shouldn't be allowed to hustle. I thought if I couldn't get what people asked for, then what is it exactly that I do? I went to the same store this time on the bus, and more importantly, alone. I bought a dime bag and quietly hinted at the counter that I wanted to ask him something without other customers hearing. "What's up lil' man?" "Can I get a quarter pound here?" "Two and a quarter ($225) you ready now?" "Next time" Needless to say we made it happen, and sparked an underground link based on trust and business. We had each other's lives in our hands making transactions in a place like that.

Let's be clear. I'm hitting the fast forward button for several reasons. The first reason is because this book is not a biography. It's not about me as much as it is about you. I'm giving you what you want, a book to better you in your business endeavors, by becoming stronger at what you're doing or about to do. The second reason is because I know the nature of a hustla. You want to get down to business, not sit around reading a novel or philosophizing. For that reason I'm leaving out a lot of my life in attempts to get down to business. Make no mistake about it, the content of my life make up the content of this book. With that being said, I will continue with my childhood resume that precedes a lot of adult ones today.

29th Street

In 1997 I was selling quarter and half pounds for twenty-five and fifty dollar profits. I was seventeen years old and was either buying sneakers or smoking up the profit. A friend of mine was selling weed at the time also, but had a friendship relationship with the connect. One day he decided to toss me the connect because he wasn't making money from these sales, that may have required a train, a pager, and some quarters for the pay phone. The connect, let's just say was an overall good dude. He's now been deported, but I can honestly say he's one of the realest businessmen that I've encountered on these streets. If there was one thing in life he knew how to do, it was hustle. He told me to come with him to the spot, which was on 29th and Girard Ave. It was a Jamaican video rental store that will definitely go down in history. I'll get back to them in a minute, for now let's focus on my face being in the place. After leaving the spot, he took me down the street to a house where he had thrown parties before. The people that lived there were in a unique situation that he tried to capitalize off of several times.

It's important for me to explain the circumstances behind this house before continuing on with this story. The house was rented to a group of people who were paying rent until one month the landlord disappeared. They started saving the money for his return but he never showed up again. After using the place to their content, the residents offered the place to another group of people to begin their rent free journey. The house was a classic three story North Philadelphia victorian house, renovated into four large apartments, equipped with lofts and spiral staircases. One day shortly after arguing with my mother about going to school or work and not hustling, I got a page from one of the residents at the house. They were offering me an entire apartment inside of the house. I wasted no time in telling them I would move in right away. Here I was being told that hustling will get me nowhere and that I had to work hard for things in life, when that thought was interrupted by an offer to live rent free with a set of spiral staircases separating the floors.

Now I'm no fool. I knew that I was being invited into this house for a reason. I'm sure they thought that I was dumb enough to believe that I was special and they were concerned about where I lived after the first time we met, but in reality I knew the truth. They knew that I was connected and figured if I moved in the weed would follow, and in this regard they were right. The day after moving in, I called and asked for a pound to sell. I was given it and told to hurry up, couple days at the most. I figured surely five people could sell sixteen ounces. This appeared to be their first time at this dance, which in my mind made it easier because they were being introduced to the game with prices that people had earn. This meant they should have easily had customers because of the low cost we were paying. The problem came in when I put a price on it. I got the pound and knew that the average ounce at the time was between a hundred and a hundred and twenty-five dollars. I told them I wanted seventy-five dollars an ounce. Two things happened as a result of this. One was those who couldn't hustle, couldn't generate customers. The other, was those who had some hustle resented my price. What they didn't understand was what I knew very well, which was my value. The fact that we had a pound of weed on the table that wasn't paid for meant that I had already delivered on my value. If something went wrong, I had to suffer the consequences. What they couldn't wrap their heads around, was me making money off of them. I grew up hustling and knew that we all have to pay someone, it's about positioning yourself correctly. If you hang around your supplier long enough you will become friends. This doesn't mean that he will decide not to profit from you anymore. On this pound of weed I was left stuck because of time constraints, and resorted to other means to pay for it that won't be discussed here.

They had actually proved my assertions correct by abandoning the deal in the middle of it. I didn't have that option. After this wild ordeal I never asked for what I couldn't move. I immediately went back to the hustle that I knew. I called everyone I used to hustle with and told them to put out the word that I was connected to all the product they would ever need. I was seventeen and on my own and desperately needed to build a business. A friend of mine from school started calling me for quarter pounds enabling me to make twenty-five dollars on each one. The good thing about it was that I only had to walk a block away to get it. The bad thing was that I had to call my connect to meet me there to take me into the spot. This spot didn't welcome everyone. You could easily get yourself shot if they didn't want you around. This particular spot was a video store that sold more pounds of weed than they rented videos. If you wanted a pound or more you would be in the back of the store in the porno section where the weed was chopped and weighed, with incense burning all throughout the store. Hundreds of pounds moved out of this spot before it was eventually shut down.

One afternoon I couldn't get my connect on the phone and desperately needed to make a sale. I decided to brave up and go in without him. I walked in and mumbled who I came there with before. They recognized me and let me purchase what I wanted while my customer was waiting in the pizza shop across the street. I was welcomed in the spot and now had my connect's connect. I knew I was in an awkward position that my old connect eventually laughed off and relieved me from. He was making plenty of money and understood that this is how the game went. If he didn't want this to happen he would have never taken me there. In a sense, it was a brave, immoral move, but it was a part of my learning curve on the street. Now that I was connected, my mistakes would be on my name, and no one could save me from the repercussions. This sharpened my blade. I began to build a relationship inside of this gangsters paradise and built a name for myself in the streets. The friends that I lived with witnessed this happening and started to realize that I was self made, opposite to what they had believed previously. With no rent to pay, the fruits of my labor became extremely visible in the house.

Two of my roommates didn't have a hustling bone in their bodies. The other two did, but allowed other things to get in the way. One was not prepared to come into the street and get dirty, which I respect him for admitting. The other allowed his ego to think for him, making him try to dictate my hustle. This is something that I couldn't tolerate, and established after the first pound of weed I brought into the house. He told me that he had a sale and could make twenty-five dollars from it. He needed me to get it, and said he would keep twenty and give me five because I was simply walking up the street. I could have easily done this for him, but didn't like the way he told me what he would give me in exchange for the service, especially offering to give me five dollars. I couldn't do this after being abandoned the first time, so I told him he had to charge his customer more next time. I knew he didn't like the idea that I was selling him weed and not sharing my connect. He told me that he was doing me a favor and that he could really just walk up the street himself. I let him do this because I simply didn't work for five dollars. Well, after he was chased out of the gangster's paradise on 29th street, my value had been solidified and never questioned again. The fact is that had the spot been raided while I was in there for him, five dollars couldn't justify that for me.

While my business began to grow, one of my roommates took notice and offered to introduce me to a friend of his in South Philly that was running an operation that he had invested in. The first day we met I was given a shot that I took full advantage of. This particular partner turned out to be a "brotha from anotha motha" that I later ended up taking over that section of the city with. I could offer him what no one else could, heart and dedication and he offered me what most people wouldn't, an opportunity. These are my humble beginnings before things got interesting. Without stretching this out any more lets jump on in and get started learning from the pros!

Lesson from 29th Street:
What Are You Worth?

The biggest jewel I can offer from this story is to know what you are worth. You must always be aware of what you bring to the table, even if you bring nothing. Knowing what you can add to a situation helps you to determine the value that you bring. There will always exist those that seek to question your value. They may have a different idea of what you are worth or may just be out to undervalue you for their own selfish reasons. You can't expect for people to opt to pay you what you're worth without you establishing your own value. It is the nature of a customer to try to get things for less than they are truly worth. Make sure that when your services and presence is brought into question you know exactly what you bring to the table, and draw clear lines in the sand of what you will and won't accept. Don't let people confuse their assumptions with actual fact, especially when speaking about your value.

Chapter Two
The Truth: You Must Be Crazy

Are you completely out of your mind? If so, then welcome. I like to be around crazy people myself, particularly those who are crazy about the success of their business. With my background in street I'm a special kind of crazy. I think I fall into the "completely out of my fucking mind" category. I like to administer to people the very same application test that in my life I've often passed with flying colors. The test is for business owners and drug hustlers alike to think of all of the things required of them to make their businesses prosper, and then formulate it into a list of job requirements. Next, write down the amount of money that they will earn and place it next to the list of requirements and other problems that they will likely encounter. Lastly, ask yourself one simple question. Does what I do now sound appealing? For the average business owner, the answer will be hell no! If you've clearly answered hell no and are going to continue on, then all I can say to you is congratulations. You are just the type of crazy ass person who can succeed in business.

The drug dealer when given this test is a special case. Their job description earns them the right to be called certified coo coo. To be called merely crazy wouldn't be at all fair to them. We translate crazy into words like determined, driven, focused, ambition, but the fact is that other people see our ways and chalk it up to one word, crazy! You have to be willing to embrace being crazy and that requires tunnel vision. The problem with tunnel vision is that it blocks the peripheral vision necessary to see things that may change things positively for you. It is sometimes wiser to modify your tunnel with peripheral windows that you can peek out of from time to time. There can be an extremely fine line between being the focused type of crazy, and the crazy type of crazy. For the sake of being completely thorough let's take that test.

The Business Owner's Sanity Test

1. The average business day consist of eight hours. Do you consistently work overtime on your business?
2. If you've answered yes to the first question, do you sometimes feel that overtime isn't enough?
3. Do you find yourself constantly thinking about your business even when you are not working?
4. Do you find yourself considering everything else in life other than your business trivial?
5. Do friends and family beg you to take days off?
6. When out with friends and family, are you really wishing that they would just allow you to get back to work?
7. Have you set only long term goals for yourself without evaluating any short term ones?
8. Do you find yourself only able to speak comfortably to those that are in your line of work?
9. Do you feel that only you can run your business, and get uncomfortable with someone filling in for you?
10. Do you feel that you are one hundred percent invested in your business and are unwilling to except advice from those who haven't commit to the level of commitment that you have?

If you have answered yes to all of these questions, you are not alone. You are a part of a small minority of people who have what it takes to make it. In my mind, the one element that differentiates the two types of crazy is growth. When you answer yes to all of the questions in this test, you are clearly in a heavy state of belief. You believe in something that others may or may not. The reason why growth is so important is because it is the physical manifestation of your belief in your business. So in essence, if answering yes is aiding you in achieving growth then you are perfectly "business" crazy. Now in the event that you answer yes to all of these questions and aren't seeing any progression in your endeavors, then perhaps its time to listen to your friends and family and go stop and smell some roses or something.

The drug dealer that answers yes to all of the above is my kind of hustler. These are the people I connect with the easiest. They are highly dedicated and focused on something illegal. This heightens their senses, giving them the uncanny ability to spot good or bad business almost instantly. When you have laser focus on a business that could land you in jail at any moment, it can render you completely out of your fucking mind! But isn't that what business is? Ideas are born inside of the minds of those crazy enough to entertain them. Crazy people see things that aren't there, and in business this can be of great benefit. Normal people walk down the same street everyday on their way to work, while us crazy folks may decide to rent out that old empty store on the route and try something new. Crazy people see things like fruit stands and food trucks parked on streets where there aren't any. This is the exact same craziness that prompts normal people to say, "What made you think to do this?" and your answer should boldly be "I'm crazy!".

Truthfully speaking, fans of Albert Einstein would be shocked to know that his definition of the word insanity proves that entrepreneurs are the most sane people walking on our streets today. He described insanity as doing the same thing over and over and expecting a different result. Aren't these the actions of those that go to the same job daily without deviation and expect life to get better? That is the wide scale level of insanity that most people live under. Then there are those that know how to direct their insanity by setting timelines and goals. They are the people that say, "I'm going to go temporarily insane". These are the crazy kind of people that influence our society. If you have the ability to look at a dilapidated building and see a beautiful flourishing business instead, most people will describe you as crazy, simply for seeing what isn't already there.

There are obviously many different degrees of crazy, so before we get too wrapped up in the word, I think it would be wise to acknowledge that at some point or another, all ten questions on the test have exhibited a characteristic of a successful person. Business school isn't going to speak about being crazy and the benefits of it, but this is the hidden jewel that lies in the minds of the successful. You may not be willing to sell drugs, and admitting that would be the smartest thing you've ever done, but when you commit to the level that I've committed to, life becomes your business school. This book might actually convince you that the convicted felon filling out an application with you, just might posses more business savvy than anyone in your company. I know this from experience. There are plenty of real life business experiences that I could have offered a number of companies that simply would not hire me.

School is a great place to learn how to structure a business, start a business, build a spread sheet, and much more. It can also provide you with information on how to purchase things, create an evaluation, and project future sales. These are all valuable assets that can add to your business's progression. However, there is the "X" factor that exists within all businesses that I have come to notice is rarely spoken of. What do you do when you've followed a plan and things are going the other way? Let's say for example you're opening a pizza parlor and have followed your plan to the letter. You've taken all the required steps from creating a business plan to securing your funding. You've found what you consider to be a prime location equipped with heavy foot traffic, top of the line equipment and all. Not to mention that perfect recipe that you've held on to is now in the oven. What does your school suggest you do with that feeling in your stomach that you get when not one customer walks into your shiny new establishment? That feeling is actually strong enough to drive you to being the real kind of crazy. I'm talking about straight-jacket, talking to yourself, nervous twitch having type of crazy.

Plenty of seminars are now telling people how easy it is to own a business and become their own boss, yet I don't recall any that attempt to give you the stomach for what you may possibly encounter. While any number of veteran hustlers and business owners alike will tell you to relax, its just the first day, it's extremely unnerving to think you've wasted a lot of your time and all of your money on something that isn't working. This mindset is poisonous and will leak into your business and destroy it. It will have you saying things like "If I don't make any money in a month I'm going to have to close". What kind of statement is this to make on your first day? All of the technical work and planning that you've done is all being brought into question after the very first day. This phenomena is very real and also very natural, but almost never spoken of. The reality of the situation is that your opening was a big day. It was a very big day, for you! It may not have been for the rest of the world. It's the consistency and foundation that you lay down that will propel your business to heights your plans couldn't project, but your dreams could.

Ask yourself, what attempts have serious business teachers made to attack the feeling of being cloned? I mean past all of that, "Imitation is the best form of flattery" bullshit. I'm talking about the feeling of spending time and money in developing a system of making money that works, only to have it ripped from you and sold by someone else. In the street this can easily lead to a gun being fired, but it's the feeling behind it that I'd like to address. I like to focus on what's really going to drive your business, and no matter how many times people say business isn't emotional, that's exactly what it is. You have to learn how to control your emotions and discern when it's time to let them loose.

Now let's apply the two previous scenarios to the Insanity Test. Imagine your wife or husband asking you to stop thinking about work and enjoy dinner on the night of your grand opening that nobody walked into. Are you insane then? Or what about when your friends and family are telling you that they see that you are stressed out and need days off, all while everything that you've worked for is being cloned by a rival business. Would that mean you're crazy? I know this is a very depressing side of business, but it is still very much a part of it, and should be addressed. Of course we like to wish each other the best and bid new entrepreneurs good luck, but it is what it is, a wish and some debatable luck. Nobody in either one of these situations wants to hear a textbook answer. It doesn't address the feeling that is attempting to consume them. When in these positions you are now at war, and war does not end by someone telling you not to think about it. That will usually lead to a head shot right between your eyes. It's actually very simple. Things that threaten your business are enemies of it and place the owner in a war where he now has no choice but to destroy the enemy to defend the business. The crazy business owner often has the advantage in these instances due to being so close to the pulse of the operation. Many times they either see it coming, or simply have a faster reaction time. Now we need to take a look at the solution for the madness and how to apply it. It's called hugging the block!

Hug Da Block

Now we're about to get down to the nitty gritty of what it's all about, the essence of hustling, Block Hugging. Every business has its first day of operation and that is not to be confused with the business's inception. I'm focusing on the moment you decide to do what you have prepared to do. While I will be using drug operations as examples, you will be learning key elements of successful business operations. In drug dealing, technically your operation began the moment you decided to secure your product. This was the inception period. However, after your product was obtained and packaged your business became operational. Hugging the block, by definition is the act of standing outside and selling drugs. To me, it's far much more than that. If you are outside hustling from twelve o'clock in the afternoon to four o'clock in the afternoon, technically if you haven't left the block than you were hugging the block from twelve to four. This is not type of dedication that could give birth to a phrase like "hugging the block". That comes when someone tries to describe someone who was relentlessly standing on the corner for hours, days, weeks and more as if they were literally hugging the pavement refusing to let it go. For instance, do you think the phrase "burning the midnight oil" came into play because it was normal to burn oil at midnight? That came before electricity when those working late into the night would burn oil lamps to see. You might be asking what does this have to do with hugging the block. I want you to see, it's the intensity of the act that created its name.

So you've got a pocket full of drugs and a street to stand on, now what? This is when you realize that opening day is the beginning of you building something. Let's look intensely at the block and see what we're dealing with. First off, drugs are being sold everyday with or without you, it's happening. You aren't known for selling drugs. How could you be on your first day? You are now branding yourself, and in business the key to that is staying still! This applies on the street corner more than anywhere. Roaming around the streets in my opinion is good for ice cream trucks and other impulse buys, but not for someone trying to brand themselves, or even more so, brand a corner.

Branding a corner takes the utmost dedication that is equivalent to an extreme case of that craziness I spoke on earlier. When you first stand on the corner that you have claimed, it hasn't been established exactly what it is you are doing yet. You may be waiting for a bus or waiting for someone to meet you. The reality is there could be a billion other things you are doing other than posting on a corner selling drugs. Branding relies on a consistency that creates reliability. You can be branded negatively or positively, but we'll get into that more specifically in the chapter on marketing. Before there is any validity to what you're doing, hundreds of busses have to go by before people understand that you are not waiting for one. Before getting down to all the aspects of business that people assume are most important, the question is "Are you even there?" If you're not on the block none of it will matter. Your business is tied to your level of commitment to being there. Others will think, "Hey its life, you've got to live.", but those who are invested mentally, live with the reality of business being their life, and living means succeeding in business. Standing on the corner alerting potential customers that you're hustling is telling them that you are reliable, showing them is being there if they choose to return.

The truth is that you may not sell a thing on your first day out. However, the day can still prove itself to be profitable for you. You might tell someone you have weed for sale and they say no thank you. Later that day or several days later someone might ask that person where to get some weed and they can point them to you, only if you're there that is. The mistake lies in thinking that the entire world is supposed to see through your pocket to the contents of it, and more so, see into your mind to read that you are willing to stand here and work vigorously on your empire. This must be shown to them. When you plant yourself on a corner, expect the roots of your labor to stretch far beyond the intersection where you are standing. Believing in a product is closely associated with believing in the person selling it to you. If someone isn't willing to stand in the same spot it questions the legitimacy of their product and can also bring down the value. Standing still is standing by your product, and if the owner isn't willing to stand by the product the customer won't either.

So let's hug the block for a minute. Here I will detail aspects of the street corner that cannot be evaded on the journey of the triumphant. Brace yourself for the ongoings of the "criminally insane" block hugger. There are several different components that must be factored into what it takes to build the block on a solid foundation. Before doing so, please allow me to reiterate how entrepreneurs of all genres and walks of life can gain from the uncut tales of street corner etiquette. How you apply the information received is solely at your discretion. The first aspect I'd like to delve into is the mind of the fearless, what it is, and why its necessary. Do your best to absorb this information and take the time to figure out the smartest way for it to be applicable in your own situations.

The Fearless

Standing on the curb selling drugs takes a great deal of bravery if not stupidity. The difference between the two is bravery is being aware of the possible negative outcomes without allowing them to deter you from reaching your goals. Instead of reassessing your goals based on fear, you will now make calculated attempts to circumvent the obstacles in the way of your progress. On the other hand, stupidity is not acknowledging those obstacles and running into them head on. The stupid face the very same obstacles as the brave without the luxury of preparation. When on the corner, the threat of eminent danger is always present. For one, we know that the police are the adversary of the hustler and this is a prominent fact that will not change, but this is the business. The hustler also has to deal with the threat of being robbed without the privilege of reporting it. Let's not forget about the customers that do not understand, nor do they care about your business or your wellbeing. These threats can defeat you mentally before you have the chance to achieve the success that you are willing to work for.

What very few hustlers understand is that you have to earn the respect of everyone, including the police. There are several fine lines that have to be walked to obtain this stature. The thought of earning the respect of the police is completely unfathomable to most people because it simply doesn't seem possible, but truthfully speaking it is possible, just only achieved when functioning at the highest level. What that means is knowing what they are looking for and being able to create a presence that will serve two masters. When police are policing a community they are at work, and most people at work are looking for ways to simplify their job to avoid working too hard. I'm going to give you three examples of how something as simple as your attire and demeanor can affect you in the workplace in very different ways.

Example #1 The Underdressed

When patrolling a neighborhood police officers encounter a variety of different types of people. In urban communities hanging outside is a normal occurrence. When looking for the easiest way to do your job, the underdressed sloppy individual provides a great opportunity for the police to simply get an easy one! Although selling drugs is not a respectable career in the eyes of law enforcement, being sloppily dressed is respected in the eyes of no one. It doesn't create the presence of business or command the much needed respect of the community to adequately perform your job. In the street this will easily work against you for several reasons. Making yourself a clear target for your adversary is never a wise thing to do. You will now become first in line when they are choosing who to arrest or harass. The arrest or harassment of someone who is poorly kept is not as disheartening as the victim of it would like to believe. This is only helping to negatively brand your corner by making it an uncomfortable place for your customers to be. It also places doubt in the mind of the customer towards the quality of your product.

For the legal business owner, this can apply to your storefront as well. Investing in a coat of paint or even a five dollar broom can bring great returns on your investment. Consider the stores around you and think of which one you would pull off of the corner to arrest or harass. Is your business sloppily dressed? Are you only concerned with the operation and not the appearance? Don't confuse your store with its environment. If the street that houses your business is dirty and full of trash, make certain that the outside of your establishment is the cleanest spot on the block. This extra effort will help to garner the respect of your community while providing your customers with enough confidence in you to continue to support your endeavors. Remember, you don't have to be a witch to know the power of a broom!

Example #2 The Overdressed

Now that we've established the dangers of corner hustling, let's talk about what the overdressed hustler can expect to encounter while trying to build his operation. I think one word will sum this up, jealousy. People often associate gold chains and nice cars to drug dealers. There is absolutely nothing wrong with buying yourself tokens of your success. If you have earned these things and have reached a comfortable financial position that has allowed you to purchase nice things for yourself, then by all means enjoy them. However, these things do not belong in the workplace. Standing on the corner continuing to sell drugs while dawning your success is not a wise thing to do. Police see this as an attack on their superiority complex. This will now bring you down to the very same level as the underdressed hustler. You have now reached the status of target, and will find yourself meeting the very same fate. Similarly to the sloppy workers on the street, the hustler dawning jewelry will find himself being arrested while staring out at a non empathetic community. In the same regard, your customers are not interested in seeing the lifestyle that they are helping you to live.

Let us now apply this principal to the legit storefront from our previous scenario. We've established the fact that the store should be well maintained. Now let's add some things into the mix. Let's park an expensive car out front and have the store's owner wear some expensive clothing.

We have now destroyed the image of the humble owner who cleans his storefront and replaced it with the image of an arrogant owner who feels that he is better than the community he serves. His customers are not questioning the quality of the product, they are now questioning the pricing and feeling like every penny they give you is a penny too much. You have now driven out the empathetic nature of the community as well as your employees. The luxuries that your business has afforded you should be enjoyed in their proper setting. Allowing expensive items to drive away business will make them much more expensive than the price you are willing to pay.

Example #3 Balance

It is now time for me to introduce you to the best friend of the entrepreneur, the iron! This tool will help you to find the perfect balance you will require to post comfortably on the block to perform your duties. All too often hustlers become consumed with their surroundings, and start to become them. It may be that they don't feel the need to look presentable in such horrid conditions, or adversely, they may be in search of instant gratification due to these very conditions. The balance can be found with the iron. Pressing your clothing provides you with the ability to be taken seriously without offending your customers and adversaries. This subtle detail places you above the slovenly worker without garnering the negative attention attributed to the flashy individuals. This gives you an unseen advantage in the business world because it is an aspect of your character that will resonate with people without allowing them to put their finger on what it is they are resonating with. The iron earns respect, while jewelry earns envy, it is completely up to you what you deem best for you.

The marriage between the business owner's appearance and their success directly correlates with the nature of fearlessness. How you present yourself can aid you in removing certain obstacles from your path. This will revolutionize the way you think and feel, and will be perceived by onlookers as fearlessness. How you see yourself, coupled with how others see you can build an aura around you strong enough to face whatever or whomever may come your way. People tend to think that one's attire should not be associated with their character, yet the reality is that characters wear clothing.

We'll discuss your product in a few of the later chapters, but for now I'd like to keep the focus on the mindset that you will need as a prerequisite to successfully hug your block. When in the correct state of mind there is little room for deviation. Dedication is something that cannot be taught or bought. It has to come from each individual with an individual application. From the outside perspective success is frequently attributed to things that have aided the successful, rather than the more important fact of what drives the successful. This point brings us to what I like to call the law of distraction, and that is, whatever you allow to distract you, will.

No Distractions

The Law of Distraction is by far easier said than done. There are some distractions in your life that you will be willing to set aside, some may prove to be much harder, and then there are those that you had no idea were distracting you in the first place. Most business owners will tell you they are one hundred percent focused on their business without being aware of the severity of what they are saying. In the event that you envision yourself running a quaint little operation that could fold at any time, or be rubbed out by a larger competitor, by all means skip this section, or better, close this book! This is for those of you who are genuinely looking to understand how to meet with your goals. Some of you will find a new energy in your life after reading this book and will try to share it with someone you are in business with. What you will find is that although some people will feel what you feel and be ready to leap from the starting block with you, there are others who will agree to the lessons in this book but won't be willing to apply them. This is the nature of the game. When hustling, allowing yourself to be distracted can quickly become your downfall. Not paying attention in the jungle is the easiest way to become food.

So what does it take to avoid your distractions? For starters, you have to know what you want, even if you don't understand the magnitude of it. In business courses, the attention is always placed on the business plan and never the business dream. The two work hand in hand. The dream is a long term goal, while the plan is used to set markers in time until reaching the finish line that is the manifestation of your dream. The beauty of the dream or long term goal is it gives the entrepreneur a point of focus that is exclusive to their own mind. Working towards your dream will yield the greatest reward because it will literally be the situation that you've dreamed of. Simply dreaming provides a powerful goal for the entrepreneur because the contents of the dream are achieved at different times creating a timeline. For example, you may have a simple dream of having your business run like clockwork. Until it does, you will be hugging the block working towards that goal. There was no plan involved, just the dedication towards seeing your vision come to fruition. The three largest distractions for the block hugger are family and friends, recreation, and doubt. Let's look further into each of these sections separately to help ensure a prosperous outcome is achieved.

Friends and Family

Friends and family can be of great benefit to a business owner when being supportive of the dream. The problem with this is that your dreams are exclusive. People can support you, not your dreams. The details of your dream are in your own head. Now while they might be playing on a never ending loop in there, that show might only play once a day in the minds of your supporters. Remembering this is the key to remaining calm when the inevitable occurs, the attempts to pull you away from your business. Family and friends can easily convolute your business practices. This takes place because they often feel that the fact that they are in support of you has been established, nothing that they do should be considered to be a distraction. This element can cause a very tense relationship between the two of you to evolve. The truth is, when it comes to your business you must be crazy, and not many people are willing to go crazy with you. That's a lot to ask of someone. The best way to handle these situations is to be perfectly clear in order to give someone a point of reference for your insane behavior. If you tell your loved ones clearly that you are getting ready to go insane for a period of time, and that things are going to be very different from how they currently are, you will find that you will be able to refer to that conversation when being confronted with your insanity. They will be reminded that you are the same family member or friend, and that your crazy behavior is all a part of your master plan.

Recreation

Do you want to be a shaky businessman in the club buying drinks? Does that sound appealing to you? How about going fishing while owning a struggling business?

Doesn't sound too great, does it? What the growing business owner has to realize is that recreation time doesn't exist for the block hugger. Recreation is for the successful! When growing a block, things are brought down to the basics. The human body needs food and rest, not recreation. It's not a requirement, nor is it a component on the road to success. If you're going to enjoy yourself, then really enjoy yourself. Don't be a shaky businessman destroying his business while building someone else's. Obtain your success first and go to the club with confidence, knowing if you wanted to, you could buy a drink for everyone in the club. That's the feeling you were looking for when you set out to grow your empire in the first place. Don't cheat yourself by feeling that you deserve a break because you have been working hard. You need to convince yourself that what you deserve is to live out your dream. The hard work that you feel you deserve a break from was all toward your own dream. Give your operation the utmost respect and attention and you will instinctively know when you've earned that recreation time your looking for. The feeling attached to fully enjoying yourself comes after you have built something, and only after its built to your satisfaction.

Doubt

The road to growing a block can be a bumpy and vigorous one. When faced with a daily adversary, you might often find yourself questioning the journey ahead. It's natural to look around at people who don't have the pressure that you have and question why it is you're doing what you're doing. This is absolutely normal, but must be tamed. At one point you were willing to leave the realm of the sane and go insane for a while. Of course you will at times question your own sanity. What you have to remember is that you are crazy, but you have intentionally gone there. Now that you've arrived you have to complete your mission to come out on the other side.

When hugging the block, it's amazing how doubt can play a role in your growth. It emanates from you. Customers don't understand your doubt. It can be misinterpreted as doubt in your product or overall business. This does not feel good to someone watching where their dollars are going. Confidence gives the impression that you are supposed to be there. It even lets your adversaries know that you are serious and a force to be reckoned with. You have to remove doubt from your mind and trust yourself. Commit to seeing your dreams materialize, and be careful not to dream too small!

Now I'd like to address the world you live in and not the world we live in. The hustler does not live on planet earth like most people would like to think. The hustler actually resides in "Block World", and that is a very different place. Right now it's time for us to park the car and get out, to take a walk through "*Block World*"

Adaptation: Your World Is The Block

What's going on in China right now? What's happening in Chicago at the moment? How about the North Pole, or even simply across town? The answer for the block hugger should be "Who gives a fuck?". Those places are all on earth, and most of the occurrences there aren't relevant in "Block World". What happens in the world is not a concern of the temporarily insane. Watching news and media outlets are for people who are not building. Of course the news will be on from time to time, and I'm not saying not to watch it. What I am saying is, it is the equivalent of watching a news station from another planet. The only part of the news that would be relevant is something that pertains directly to you or your situation.

When hugging the block, everyone around you will become your news. You will be listening to the street. You are watching and listening to the street because this is where your business is and the news you hear applies to your business. Foreign affairs and pop news is all useless on the block. The knowledge that matters on the street directly effects the business. In "Block World" what I don't know is the ongoings of the things that are relevant to earthlings. What I do know is every face that comes around the block, as well as every car. I can tell you what they are doing on the block and know whether they present a threat or not. I know when the police are watching from blocks away because that is the station that I am tuned into. I'm not busy watching news and television shows. I'm watching the street, and watching my enterprise grow. This is what staying informed means here.

Some people will say that it is reckless to not be concerned with the events in the world. To that, I can only say this. It may be reckless in your eyes, but do you think a temporarily insane resident of "Block World" gives a fuck what you think is reckless? The block hugger at all times must keep a level head in their world, not in the world that others want them to live in. The stakes are high in business so the more you know, the better off you will be. The information just has to be relevant to your business. For example, the weather in "Block World" is much different from the weather on earth. Do you think the police don't know what you're doing standing on the corner in the rain? To an earthling, it's just raining. In "Block World" the rain could expose you in a different light. Now in the case that you are driving to deliver large amounts of drugs, the rain can be your friend. Police officers aren't looking to get wet while pulling you over, creating and opportunity for safe deliveries. These are two adverse affects of the very same rainfall. Learning your world is the deciding factor in progressing from the block and back into reality.

This concept is very similar to a soldier at war. The soldier wants to come home and enjoy his family, yet has to first make it out of the war surrounding them. Your business is in a warlike setting, and there are several things around that threaten the success of your business. Just like the soldier, you have to focus on the war and not your home. Focusing on the war around you is the only way you are going to make it home. The thought of making it home should remain on your mind, but what's going on at home will get you killed on the battlefield. The war zone is very similar to the block in that regard. The soldier doesn't have the luxuries that the citizens do, just as the hustler or business owners don't either. They have to fight the war to grow the business, and that takes a mental investment. They have to focus on where the enemy is, destroy it, and secure their victory.

Ok so let's take a look at what we've created here. We now have an extremely determined, focused, and fearless hustler, who has dedicated themselves to the business and to mastering their environment, all while being dressed for the part. With this formula it won't be long before what we see standing in front of us is success. With this new found success comes new faces, as well as old faces that want to partake in your new found success. After all that has gone into what you've constructed, it's time to learn the value of sweat equity.

Sweat Equity On The Block Is Invaluable

Now we are standing in a very different place. After following all of the previous steps to applying the energy and effort to gaining a firm grip on your business, you will find yourself moving ahead in your venture. A lot of people will think that you owe them, or may simply want a job. By now you know your business like the back of your hand. Most importantly you know who built your business. When you reach the point where your business is rolling, you must now evaluate your sweat equity, and in the street the price is high. In the beginning of this chapter we spoke on going crazy. Now that you have gone crazy and are reentering the realm of sanity, trying to put a price on that is not an easy thing to do. How much does it cost to go crazy? You may think that you will never have to answer this type of question, but these are the types of questions that surround success.

There are several different ways your sweat equity can be challenged, possibly by a friend that doesn't quite understand what you've been willing to endure. It may even come from a new employee that doesn't grasp how much you put into developing the business. All they are concerned with is a wage increase. All of your sleepless nights, and early mornings mean nothing to them. Those whom may have watched alongside of your journey may even feel a degree of envy. This type of envy can come from someone closely associated to you who may be in admiration of what they've witnessed you do. In the end, people must respect the work that you've put in. In order for them to know how much, you must first know how much.

Sweat equity in essence is your "shit talking rights". That is when you're able to talk shit and back it all up. With some people it will be the first time they find out about all the labor and dedication it took for you to build your business. In the same vein, you will see those that know exactly what they've watched you build and can't believe that you're speaking on it. This is something that you must never disregard. This is who you are. If there are things in life that build character, then building the block is definitely one of them. The holidays that you've skipped, the good times with friends that you've missed, all holds value. The beautiful part of this is that you set your own value, and only you are in control of how you relinquish it. The sweat equity earned from the block is invaluable in many ways, so you should be mindful of how you let go of it.

Real Life Application: The Building Blocks of Building a Block

Some people are fascinated by the four corners of the Earth. For me, for a long time my fascination lied with the four corners of the intersection of 5th and Reed St. in South Philly. While other spots and corners I had partaken in my life had endowed me with some very influential life lessons, what my partner and I had accomplished on 5th street became the blueprint for all of my future endeavors. This is the type of drive that will enable you to move forward in ways that you couldn't possibly imagine. Make sure to stuff your pockets with all of the jewels dropped in this story of a "Block Hugger".

In the early part of the year 2000, a good friend of mine saw me in the early stages of building a block in North Philadelphia. The early stages of building a block were always rough, but he could see that no matter how much work I would apply, the location was not going to yield the best possible results. It would be a matter of time before I landed myself in a jail cell for setting up shop where I didn't belong. Part of him was trying to save his friend from an early demise, and part of him was trying to bring in a partner with value into his operation. Nevertheless, one day he talked me off of my corner, to a corner in South Philly, where he lived with his girlfriend. I was reluctant, but desperate, and knew that we could do what we've once done before. I then decided to regroup and head to South Philly to start from the bottom.

When I arrived on the corner of 5th & Reed St. all I could think was "He has no idea how serious I am right now." My friend had also approached another friend of ours to pull him into the operation. He was someone that I hadn't done business with before, besides a few minor transactions in the past and wasn't my main concern. On the day of our initial meeting we sat, smoked, and attempted to address the only issue that mattered, dedication. Everything else was the easy part. We knew how to hustle, we just had to commit so that we could rely on each other without thought. This was the only way this endeavor could leave the ground.

The three of us sat in my friends third floor apartment and decided to solidify our commitments by putting our money where our mouths were at that very moment. The three of us put together had a net worth of under a thousand dollars, and decided to put up two hundred and thirty-three dollars each, to invest in our futures. We had just enough money to buy a half pound of weed, the packaging for it, and a scale, rendering us now broke, but in business. The only rule we set in place was that we would not take out any money until we had reached the goal of thirty-thousand dollars, ten thousand each. We had complete confidence in our ability to make this happen. After putting our funds together my friend told us what we all knew, which was we couldn't sit in his apartment and move product. He showed us that the second floor apartment that had a perfect view of the corner was now vacant, and that the lock was mysteriously open making it accessible to us. We all agreed that we would carefully use this place for packaging product and viewing the corner when not standing on it. Standing in that second floor apartment was a nerve racking thing to do. You could literally feel the sense of breaking and entering being added to our list of potential charges.

My friend had a few customers calling his phone for product, which gave us a small platform to build from. As the calls came in, I would literally dart to the customer, but wouldn't leave them without telling them that they could always find us on 5th & Reed. A few days had gone by when I decided I wasn't going to keep traveling back and fourth between North and South Philly to work. I had a trash bag full of clothes and decided that I now lived in our stolen apartment. Every morning we would grab a newspaper to see if the place that we had taken over was still listed for rent. I found myself overwhelmed with daily relief in the evening hours, fully aware that at any given time during the daylight hours a real estate agent could be walking through the door with a client to show the apartment. By now you should begin to understand just how crazy the author of this book really is.

I decided that the confines of that second floor apartment was a luxury that we couldn't afford and began hugging the block. From early on I would look out of the window spotting someone who was selling crack about a half a block away from us. Although our businesses weren't intertwined, I knew that I was learning a great deal from watching him. The first thing that we noticed was that he would wear the same clothes everyday, faithfully. This made him a clear target who could be described by his clothing without fail. He looked like what he was, a crack dealer, one that was now wearing a uniform. The second thing that we noticed was his dedication. He would be out from dawn to dusk, everyday, uninterrupted. I could never forget the feeling that I got from watching him from the window, giving an embarrassed smile to the school children on there way to school, and how the children were told not to speak to him. I fully understood how to adapt. I learned to watch the children pass to go to school, and immediately come outside to start my day. That small amount of respect that I showed the community would go a long way.

I would now be visible on the corner from 8:00 am until midnight. Then I would go in and retire into my stolen haven until morning. This was the kickstart that we needed to stamp the block. While my partners were hugging the block with me, they simply weren't willing to come out as early or stay out as late as faithfully as I was. The early morning sales were far and few between. One of my partners didn't see the value in all of us being there. It was this dedication that forced one of my partners into feeling that his presence wasn't needed as much as it was in the beginning. This initiated the slacking off mentality. I started noticing that from 8:00 am to 9:00 am, I was on my own, and as days went by the time would push later and later with a man missing. For me, I couldn't care less because nothing was going to stop me. I was going to stand on that corner with or without help and split the money like we had agreed to.

The energy we applied to the corner turned our two hundred and thirty-three dollar investments into about thirteen hundred dollars each during the course of just over a week. It was about a week after that, that my partner came to me one morning and said that he was amazed at how business was picking up and believed that he could do the same thing across town in North Philly near his house. I couldn't believe his optimism. What he didn't know, but what I knew very well, was that he thought that he could rebuild in North Philly what he didn't build in South Philly. The traffic coming to the block was due to the dedication placed on growing it. I hadn't left the four corners at all, and hadn't planned to until we hit the thirty-thousand dollar goal that we set out for. I was insane! I figured it was probably just a thought that he was having until later that day a meeting was called, and a third of everything that we had was cut out and given to our former partner. I can never forget thinking, "That's it? You want to leave with this and start over?" Although we were approaching several weeks in, the bulk of that money was generated in the last week of business. He was opting out just before the explosion.

The next month the business did just that, exploded, and continued to maintain consistent growth. It was now time to remove all the fear from our minds completely and rent the place legally to avoid someone renting the location of our blossoming enterprise. Yes, I was crazy enough take a few dollars and live in a place until I had enough money to rent it legitimately. I was also crazy enough to succeed. I went into the office to rent the apartment with the money order made and was asked by the woman "Don't you want me to show you the apartment?" I was so flustered I told her "I'm sure its fine, I know the area." I was just there to tie the knot with the building. I was now a resident, and sitting on the steps is what residents do. Those steps later became some of the most valuable real estate in South Philly.

The intersection had a laundromat, a corner store, an Asian market and our business. We ran our building like a machine, that eventually shot past our expectations. We employed all of the tactics that I've spoken on in this chapter garnering a real presence in the community. Sweeping the trash from the corner was a daily routine. The ironing of my clothes became a morning ritual as well. Neighbors would see two guys taking care of their neighborhood while making a few extra dollars. What they wouldn't see is two hustlers tearing the community apart. There were times when the police would ride by and nod their heads in approval while we were sweeping the corner. Of course there were also times when they would sit and interrupt business, to maintain their own respect. One morning I will always remember is when all four corners were being swept by their respective business owners, myself included. I swept the outside of an illegal enterprise and was accepted as a peer amongst the owners of the corner.

Our business soared far beyond the ten thousand each we set out for, giving us the ability to occasionally seek out recreation comfortably. Venturing off of the corner that I hugged so closely, I would see our product's packaging all over the streets. We couldn't help but to laugh at our initial investment and how crazy we were. We had no plan, only dedication. We would see friends of ours in the clubs occasionally who saw their friends who were missing in action return with pockets full of money and smiles on their faces, but who also had work to do in the morning. After buying several rounds at the bar, that work was never questioned again.

Lessons from story

Lesson One:
Don't Be Tickled By Your Dreams

One of my partners walked out too soon. He didn't realize that he had only gotten a taste of the success that we were looking to achieve. Coming from being as broke as we were that taste was enough to intoxicate him. It was far too early. We hadn't even secured our location correctly at this point in time. Make sure that in your business you don't try to enjoy the mere sign of success. That feeling is a distraction from reaching the real destination which is freedom. You won't have to convince yourself that you are free. There will be nothing in your way rendering the feeling obvious. Celebrating early creates detours and roadblocks on the road to freedom.

Lesson Two:
Earn Your Respect

Earning your respect comes from following through on your vision. It comes from going above and beyond what is required of you. Picking up a broom extended our run on the block. Being orderly and presentable also aided in our prosperity. You have to create a business aura around all aspects of your business. Make people take you seriously, even when you don't know that they are looking. Respect comes from your actions and the presentation you give. Someone crazy enough to work for their dreams commands respect. Our business grew to make more than all of the other businesses on the corner and we earned the respect of the owners as they watched it grow.

Lesson Three:
Get Back To Work

After achieving our goals and setting a few new ones, we found ourselves back in the clubs for some enjoyment. It was apparent that we were not the same kids that they remembered. This feeling of enjoyment would spill over into the next morning. While it may be acceptable once in a while, you have to keep in mind why it is that you can enjoy yourself so much. What is paying for this enjoyment? The business that you have built is footing the bill. After all is said and done you have to get back to work. Slacking off will effect your future growth as well as what you've already built. It is the equivalent of celebrating too early. Be mindful not to undo all that you've worked so hard to achieve. Sometimes lightning doesn't strike twice!

Summary

Hug your block! If you are a store owner, baker, doctor, or mechanic, hug your block. Don't think that there is such a thing as being too dedicated. Stay physically and mentally invested in your business. Tune everything out to create a wall around you. Those on the inside of your wall will understand the confines of it. They will know that you are focused, and to be around you is to be excepting of that. Those who remain on the outside of your wall, belong there! They are the people in your life that fall into the category of distractions, and have to be treated as such. Part of owning a business is being able to delegate. Delegate responsibility, power, money, and people. The earlier you come to grips with this the better.

Firstly and lastly, don't be afraid to go crazy! You can't allow others to decide what's crazy for you. I think skydiving and roller coasters are crazy, but a lot of people enjoy them. Only you will know when you've gone too far. That is when you will make the necessary changes. I knew it was crazy to hustle from a stolen apartment, but I didn't think it was too crazy to be done. I took the risk and reaped the rewards. You have to be crazy in the world of business. Think about it like this. Would you rather make some money? Or would you rather make an insane amount of money?

Chapter Three:
The Art of Consignment:
Best Friend or Worst Enemy?

Consignment by definition is: The act of placing an object in someone's possession, while retaining ownership of the object until the item has been sold and the consignor has been paid by the consignee.

This can be your best friend or your worst enemy, depending on how you apply it in your own situation. The key is to remember the consignor is still the owner of the product and in most cases acts as the boss with you being the employee. This is not the only way to function. In fact the best consignment relationships are partnerships where each party is equal. This can only occur when the consignee operates like a well oiled machine and holds up his end of the bargain in royal fashion.

Consignment in its correct manner starts off with either an offer or a ticket. The drug game, due to its presence in the poorest of environments is one of the only businesses to implement the offer. Most businesses require the ticket before accepting any business from you.

The Offer: A Dealer offers you a position as a dealer and offers to supply you on a consignment basis. The other type of offer is where you offer your services to become a dealer and it is up to the dealer whether he will accept your offer and set you up with a consignment.

The Ticket: The ticket is as simple as it gets. It represents buying your way into the game the same way you buy your way into an amusement park, or a basketball game. It could be a twenty-five dollar quarter ounce or a three thousand dollar pound of weed, but the ticket represents you buying your way into the game.

Allow me to explain in detail the proper etiquette for the offer. The two types of offers should be treated in the same fashion. This is the only way to achieve an equal partnership between the Hustler and the Connect. When you enter the game on an offer, you are coming in on the lowest level and you have to act as if you are trying to climb the ladder. The best way to climb the ladder is to recognize your position at the bottom of it. All too often I've seen hustlers strutting around sticking their chest out while walking around with a pocket full of the connect's money. Just because when you were hired no one was holding a clipboard and you didn't sign anything, doesn't mean you shouldn't respect the corporate structure. Fake hustlers always find comfort in bullshitting. This is a blunt way of putting it, but the fact of the matter is that is the best way to define a poor consignment relationship. Either the connect is too demanding or the hustler/employee is bullshitting.

The process begins by not allowing yourself to get in too far over your head, especially in the street where consequences can be deadly. When dealing in consignment it is always best to request no more than fifty percent more than the necessary amount, any more should be offered and not requested. For instance, if you have sales lined up that add up to ten sold, you shouldn't be requesting any more than fifteen. This ensures that you have room for more customers to call and most importantly you can give the connect over sixty-five percent of the money owed to them as soon as it comes in, and being as though the sales are already on the way your connect can rest easier knowing that the bulk of his money has already returned home. This will help to ensure a healthy consignment relationship.

For those of you reading this who don't see the importance of this issue, you should ask yourself one simple question. "Who the fuck do you think you are?" This question should be more than simply asked and answered. It should be reflected upon for a significant amount of time. The answer to this question can be the deciding factor of your fate in the drug game, as well as any legitimate business setting. You should actually take time and assess your life situation before proceeding.

If you were in dental school, I don't think that you should be there contemplating whether or not you want to be a dentist. By the time you enter dental school the decision should have already been made. The same applies to the drug game. If you have made or accepted an offer without deep reflection, then you are in dental school and haven't decided whether you want to be a dentist or not. When you act in this manner you are quite possibly wasting the time of several different people. First and foremost you are wasting the time of your connect. Secondly, you are wasting the time of a serious applicant who could be in your spot, and thirdly you are wasting your own time. The wasting of time falls in that very same order in terms of severity. The term "the streets are watching" is an extremely important and an equally true one. Watching someone toying around in the work place creates anger and resentment which could very well bring about your early demise.

I will ask this question again so that you can fully understand its depth. "Who the fuck do you think you are?" Some people actually believe that it is ok for them to have the connect waiting and waiting like a bill collector. They don't realize that the bill collector isn't going to kick your front door in when you least expect it. In other businesses, when you are hired you signed forms and agreements to comply with the rules and regulations of the business. In the street there are no forms to sign and no list of regulations, yet when you make or accept an offer you have already agreed to the terms. Although there is no list of regulations either, the rules do exist and will be enforced. Failure to comply with the rules in an ideal situation would result in you simply being fired and having to search for a new connect. In an extreme case and depending on how flagrant the violation your loved ones could have to identify your body at the morgue. The latter scenario usually follows someone who never took the time to reflect on who they were, just as the person who flunks out of dental school probably should have decided who they were to establish a position.

Establishing a position is in other words coming to grips with your reality. It's saying my connect and I are not equal. This is not to say that you will never be, but it is rooting yourself in reality, and this is the safest place to be in the drug game. I'm certain plenty of people have fallen off the map while living in an extended kingpin daydream. If you reflect deeply on your status you will be able to affectively climb the ladder because you have come to grips with the fact that you are at the bottom of the totem pole. Once this reality sets all the way in, there is no place to go but up, and each move should be a calculated attempt to do so. More than anything, establishing your position at the bottom helps you to apply the proper focus needed to advance in this game.

For the hustler truly interested in advancing, this is where your story begins. This is that defining moment in your career where you come face to face with yourself in the mirror and say, "I ain't shit right now, but not for long!" This moment I like to refer to as your "Clark Kent moment". It is at this point when you become Clark Kent.

You have the mindset of Superman, yet all people will see is Clark. You have to perform your duties under these pretenses before you can establish yourself as a solid character. Just as Clark must learn to maneuver through the world, knowing that buried under the exterior of an average Joe is a far greater force waiting to be unleashed. You must do the same. This is the key to consignment because it creates the attitude required to endure as "Clark". Believe it or not, establishing your position at the bottom is the fastest way to get to the top!

For those of you saying to yourself "Is this guy really telling me to chill at the bottom?" Well, all I can say to you is good luck! When you choose to root yourself in something other than reality, luck is all you can rest on. The streets are very similar to the corporate structure in that entry level means entry level. It is not based on how much money you have or who you're related to. It doesn't show bias to gender or race. Although all of those scenarios can be present, none can save you in an aggressive business setting, whether corporate or street.

Entry level is where you are being watched intensely, even if you don't realize that this is the case. It can be utterly amusing to watch someone who never admitted to their self that they are employed in a consignment relationship, get fired. In many companies you are referred to as the "walking dead". These are the people that walk around all day doing their job as normal, and have no idea that the decision has already been made to terminate their employment. I used to ask myself, how could the boss be so cruel as to let them work the entire day, and then just before its time to leave call them into the office to fire them? It wasn't until I was placed in this very situation on the boss' side of the scenario when I realized just how easy it is, and what made it so effortless.

What I had to learn is what everyone in business must learn. Everyone has a part to play, and when you don't play your part the company suffers. The fact of the matter is, when you have an employee who knowingly is not meeting the companies standards or requirements, they are actually doing the very same action as the boss in the previous scenario. Everyday they come to work and bullshit their way through the day, and when its time to leave they walk past their boss' office, smile, and say, "See you tomorrow". This is precisely why the termination of their employment comes so effortlessly, and also why the boss loses no sleep before, or after letting them work their last day totally unaware of what's to come. The fact of the matter is it's actually an enjoyable experience to fire someone so deserving. They have been getting over on you with an inadequate performance for weeks, possibly months, and it's finally come to your attention. Relish the moment! Savor it, and most importantly, study it.

Once you find yourself in this position, studying your employee can be of great benefit. Some will say that's the type of information you can't buy, but they are incorrect in that way of thinking. When confronted by this particular situation you have already paid for your course by the actions that led you into this scenario. Lessons that have been paid in blood are known to be the most effective, yet the ones that touch the pocket can at times be equally effective. When watching the mannerism of your employees it is important to realize that you are in school. You may be spending money on someone unworthy. This in turn places you in a learning environment, and depending on the attention you give to the scenario you could have an extremely costly semester on your hands. Watching others behavioral habits is one of the best ways in which a person can learn without suffering from their own costly experiences.

The correct way to deal with the offer relies completely on the attitude of the consigned. This is the foundation of the relationship. It is based off of a respect level that must be maintained to ensure that the fundamental principals can be applied. It often boils down to being aware of your position in life. This brings me to my next point, Man vs The Machine.

Man vs The Machine

From the initial invention of machines they've been here to serve one purpose and that is to make life easier for humans. Out of fear of insignificance, man has often cheered for humans to win this battle. Well, I've got news for you. Your connect is always rooting for the machine. Humans have problems just as machines do, but humans have a number of excuses that machines don't. Think about it like this, if you choose not to answer your phone, the answering machine will. It doesn't go through emotions that can affect other people, nor does it decide when is the right time to pick up. The more you understand this concept the better off you will be.

This is a fundamental principle in business. Imagine if your car could talk. Picture yourself getting into your car on Monday morning to start your work day and your car refuses to start. You make other arrangements to get to work, show up late, or possibly miss the day all together. Later that day you start your car and the car tells you it was tired from driving late the night before. This would defeat the purpose of relying on machines, and let's face it, man wants machines to work for him. When the answering machine was invented it added a sense of comfort into people's lives. It allowed them the freedom of leaving their homes and trusting that their calls would not go ignored. When dealing in consignment it's your obligation to become the machine. To make it simple, Answer Your Phone!

Answering the phone is the easiest step you can take to becoming the machine you need to be. Do not confuse this with "ass kissing". Taking the connect's calls simply adds them the comfort of the answering machine. When you have several outlets to choose from, you will always go in the direction that lets you sleep at night. The person who doesn't answer the phone is the same as the car that doesn't always start. It leaves the owner in search of a new machine, and this is the last place you want the mind of your connect to roam. Always answering your phone can put you at an advantage over others even if you don't move product as quickly. Would you rather go to sleep hoping you wake up on time, or rest easy knowing the alarm clock will ring? If your supplier is not in town or leaving town, don't you think it would be wise for him to leave product with the most communicative customer? The answer to this question can help determine where you fall in line on your connect's list of priorities.

The Personality of a Robot

This aspect of Man vs The Machine is a very subtle component that when applied places you even higher on that priority list I spoke of earlier. It falls in line with the negatives of doing business with friends and family, but goes a step further. When recognizing man's need for the reliability of machines, this will inevitably lead you to the issue of getting personal. Doing business with friends and family is a recipe for disaster. It may often seem like a good idea especially when dealing with illegal substances because it provides some level of comfort that all connects are in search of. The downside is that this is the furthest thing from a machine that you can find, it has a personality.

The friend or family member that is consigned has a much more powerful arsenal of excuses to confound your business. They have the ability to mix sentiment in where it doesn't belong. It is natural for them to assume that they're entitled to discounts and special treatment. I mean after all, you can't possibly charge me what you charged him, right? Wrong! Friends and family shorten the necessary margins needed to grow small businesses. They sometimes choose to insert old memories into the present days business settings. When waiting on a friend or family member to pay a business debt, the phone call is much different from the call of someone you don't have a personal relationship with. The conversation often begins with something personal and ends with something personal. It defies the machine like qualities that you are looking for when in a consignment agreement, leading to the worst feeling in business, losing a friend.

It is my professional opinion that the worst of all of these traits is the ability to play the victim. Friends and family use this all too often, and the fact of the matter is that victims take victims! The friend victim confuses business with calling on or receiving help from a friend. The two are opposites because the friend of business is business, and its arch enemy is friends and family. These are the people that feel that their personal problems trump yours, your business and anyone else's. First, they will take the "need a friend" approach, pouring out their heart like a friend in need. The friend approach is always the easiest because it tares apart the senses. It makes the good friend come to the victim's aid. Next comes the ask. Here's when the answer to your friends problem becomes doing business with you. Because the lines have been blurred, if you decline the ask, you are not declining business, you are turning your back on a friend in need. Do you see how tricky this can be? You have one friend saying to himself "How could he do this to me? He knows I'm running a business!", with the other friend saying, "Why is he stressing me? I'm your friend, you know I will pay!" The friendship as well as the business has been strained. The best way to deal with a friend in need is friend to friend, not friend to business owner.

Now I'd like to take it a step further by showing you how the rule of not doing business with friends and family applies to everyone you deal with. The nature of business demands attention. When doing business, you have to be aware of those who talk too much before getting down to business. This can happen even while doing simple transactions. Often what's happening is someone is attempting to create a false friendship very quickly, and may very well lead to the same outcome of doing business with a friend. I'm not saying friendships don't occur in business. My closest friends were made through business, but it will always be the elephant in the room. You have to remove the business from the room before being friends. You have to be aware of the line between being cordial and entering a false friend zone. Ask yourself why is someone you only have a business relationship with telling you personal things about their life before doing business? They are quite possibly setting up the friend or victim status, and that can alter the course of business for you. Its better to be upfront about your business and aware of these types of people. Remember you know who your friends are. Don't let business associates fool you!

Pay Like An ATM

When you enter a consignment agreement you are now in the automatic teller machine business. That's right you've turned yourself into an A.T.M. Here we are again at the point where the ego driven individual says enough of this guy's ass kissing and here we are again at the point where I remind you that you're getting ready to piss off a connect and not make any money. You have to make it as simple as that. You must recognize that as long as you have product that is not paid for, you don't have money. It's a very simple concept. If you want to hold money, then simply pay what you owe and hold your own money, but when your connect is asking for money, after all it is theirs. Pay like an A.T.M.! Your money will always continue to grow if you are continuously supplied. Now there is such a thing as an overbearing connect who is too demanding. This isn't to be confused with your A.T.M.-like abilities. When your connect asks you for a payment in between payments, he is offering you leverage. He is extending an opportunity for you to respond as more than a customer but as a partner. Although it may not be what you had planned to do that day, it may lead to much better days for you.

Count your money and pay how the machine pays. If the machine says it gave you five hundred dollars and spit out four hundred and eighty-seven dollars, that would destroy our faith in the reliability of these machines everywhere. Having to sit in car with drugs in it counting money because of a lack of trust, can be extremely similar to wondering if the check someone is giving you is payable. Sometimes the A.T.M. will run out of funds but it will tell you it is out of funds. This also leans into the rules of communication. People who are not honest about paying in shorts give the feeling of using a broken A.T.M. daily. Eventually you are going to look for a new machine to go to.

I think what I like best about an A.T.M. is that they don't party, and they don't pay bills. They leave your money alone until you come to pick it up. You don't go to the machine to take out money to pay a bill and hear that the machine doesn't have it because it just paid a bill. I could imagine how many broken machines we would find if people were putting their cards in and receiving slips with excuses on them. "Sorry insufficient funds, partied it."

"Sorry insufficient funds, paid my phone bill." I'm sure these machines would be ripped to shreds sooner or later. Now, would you like your connect to think of you in terms of if you were a machine he would rip you to shreds?

Real Life Application of Healthy Consignment: My Connect with No-Name

This is the story of my connect with no name. No, I am not protecting his identity, I literally called him No-Name. This is the perfect situation to explain a great consignment relationship because I received over fifty pounds of weed from this guy before I knew his name, purely from doing great business. No-Name was for lack of better words a wild Jamaican with a much wilder reputation. It was much later that I found out that he was really more of a robber than a hustler, and that most of what I sold for him was stolen from other hustlers, some of whom I had become good friends with later in life. He was a shooter and in the Jamaican community in Philadelphia and New York his name rang out as a Shotta.

I met No-Name one day when an older friend of mine handed me his phone and said, "Tell this guy I'm not here and I forgot my phone." I did what he asked and No-Name gave me an ear full of some choice words for my friend and his mother. Waiting for money is no picnic. I happened to be at the next spot when he came for his money. My friend was a little bit leery of his volatile ways and decided to slow down on taking things from him. He remembered my name from the phone call and trusted me for some reason, even though he knew I was lying to him on the phone. I told him I wanted to buy a pound of weed, and he told me to call him and meet him in an hour. When I met up with him he took the money I had and said, "Here's five". This guy was truly out of his mind, but it was just the kind of person I needed. Not only was his product better than most, but it was cheaper too. I guess you can do that when you purchase it with a gun in somebody's face.

He would call me all times of day with the shortest notice possible wanting me to meet him in all sections of the city. To me it was all apart of the day. Any time he called I answered. Taking him whatever I had whenever he asked. Day in and day out we started to roll. I had a heavy connect and word started moving. I began getting sales for three to five pounds and started seeing him more often. Before long he was throwing me fifteen pounds at a time. All I had to do was answer my phone. There were some cases where he needed to take back one or two from me to sell on his own. I would jump in the car to meet him, knowing that I was now working for free. It didn't matter, all that did was make him feel like he had a partner rather than a worker. Workers get disgruntled while partners aid the mission at hand. It didn't matter to me if I had to bring the money to him or wire it to Jamaica, I was now a machine he could rely on.

After a few short yet profitable months, he had me start meeting him at his house where he showed me his arsenal, basement full of dogs, and also played some music that he made. All this despite the fact that nobody is supposed to know where a robber lives. It was obvious to him that all I cared about was more weed, not telling stories, lying, ducking phone calls, or women problems, just more weed. I gave him whatever money I had, to me my money was weed. I would keep just enough money to live and give him the rest. My money was all product. If need be I would sell a pound and put a thousand in my pocket. It was this way of being that prompted him to show the ultimate act of trust. He was going to Jamaica, well at least he said he was and asked me to watch his house. He gave me the keys to his house, car, and access to more guns than I would ever need. I mean he showed me multiple hand guns, assault rifles and more. He attempted to show me how they worked but I just didn't care. All I could smile about was the sixty pounds of weed he left in the basement, hell yeah!

While he was gone things turned up for me. I made a sale for twenty pounds at once that left me smiling. My phone was ringing left and right, for single pound sales that I welcomed. One day an associate of mine who also sold weed, stepped out of town and asked me to handle his customers for the day. This was one of the busiest times I can remember, leaving me without a second to spare. It was one of those moments in time that reminds you how deep your dedication lies. Throughout the week I transferred the product to my house treating No-Name's place as my own in his absence. He would have never been running in and out of his house all day with bags and boxes so I didn't either. It made more sense for me to conduct business in my usual fashion to secure the both of us. Treating his house in any other way could have resulted negatively for us unexpectedly, and this is what I was entrusted with.

Early the next week without warning I received a call from No-Name saying he was back in town and had given me his only key to his house. I met up with him in the street and gave him his key. When he reached his house I received a flaming hot phone call from him enraged that he had no product, in other words, panicking. I told him everything was cool and attempted to explain to him I had the money and he immediately calmed down and shut down the conversation. The next morning I took him over forty-seven thousand dollars and had the remaining seven pounds in my house. I'm not sure what impressed him more, the fact that so much was sold or the fact that his house was in the exact same mess that he left it. All I did was take the weed and stop in to feed the dogs, but in the street that's not easy to find.

That day he asked me to take a ride with him so he could get me thirty more and I was more than willing. I knew that I would now be getting the bulk of his weed and that him asking me to take the ride was a personal gesture because he could have easily gone to get it himself. These rides create power links. Having your face amongst prominent people means a lot. That day we went to a junkyard where he had some type of arrangement to have his product towed into the lot in the trunk of an old car. After getting it into his truck we stopped by a Jamaican mechanic shop that happened to be owned by a friend of mine. I saw dealers that had supplied me in the past who were all wondering what we were doing together, while knowing the answer. While No-Name was off running his mouth somewhere, my old friend who had almost twenty years on me approached the car and said "You riding with him? Careful Jus..." I took heed to what he was saying but realized, I know the guy with four pit bulls who likes to make music and ride dirt bikes. You guys know the wild shooter that gives out leg shots to people that owe him money. I do good business and others don't, so we know two different people.

Lessons from story

Lesson One:
Communication

There is a lot to be said for communication. It was my friends lack of communication that prompted me to meet No-Name in the first place. To him entertaining a girl that was only with him because of the money she was now preventing him from making, was more important than communication with his connect. This is not the side of a wild shooter you want to be on. In business, communication is protocol. It's fundamental in any business, anywhere. You have to be accessible. This is why doctors initially had pagers, and then drug dealers, onto the rest of the world. Everyone in business has to be able to be contacted. All to often people try to assume what someone is calling for and determine if the call should be answered. This will lead to the exact opposite of a positive consignment relationship and a lack of trust. Think about it, consignment is trust, so doing things that weaken trust, weaken consignment. Business isn't like it is in the movies. There is no one boss or wizard of Oz. Everyone relies on each other and those who are the most reliable flock together to build stronger networks.

Lesson Two:
Recognize Your Employment

From the time I took the five pounds of weed from No-Name I was employed. This was a fact that I faced head on. There would be no benefit in denying that fact. That employment was under my control. If I were to treat it in any other way, it wouldn't have been possible to achieve success. People tend to believe that you are some how reducing yourself to an errand boy or someone answering to the connect's every beckoned call. It is this illusion that clouds the mind of a business person and takes on a life of its own, one that is rooted in a false reality. This negative way of looking at things is the fire that burns the bridges that you need to cross. Communication is something that must be equally sided. People who are waiting for their consignment are eager to answer their phone. After receiving their consignment, they should be just as eager to answer the phone and communicate with the real owner of the product.

Lesson Three:
Respect Affiliate Businesses

Business can create a very selfish environment and set of circumstances around you. It often comes down to the level of respect that we exhibit to one another. Caring for the business of those you are in business with is key. You have full knowledge of what it takes for your business to succeed. Having knowledge of what others around you need will also help your business to grow. Sometimes you have to help someone to help you. The fact of the matter is that business owners are sensitive people. They can easily pick up on things that will hurt their business and those who are not concerned with their progression. While focusing on others progression should not be first and foremost, it is a relevant factor in the growth of your business. Simply put, people are not willing to watch your business grow at the expense of their own. You can't put a strain on someone so that only you can prosper. If you don't respect that your connect has the very same problems that you do, you will soon find yourself in search of a new connect. Bills, deadlines, and someone else to answer to exist in all businesses, and acknowledging that fact will only strengthen the relationship between the consigned and the consignor.

Real Life Application of Poor Consignment: The Tale of "Jo"

There are many examples of negative consignment relationships in my life, most of them are the inspirations for writing this book. The one that sticks out the most to me is the story of "Jo". If this story sounds familiar to you perhaps you've seen his face plastered all over the news for having his uncle killed during a home invasion in a

Pennsylvania suburb. If you haven't seen the news broadcast with him, then maybe you've seen the episode on him that was featured on a show that details the circumstances around high profile murder cases. Nevertheless I'll explain to you my dealings with this guy as he was once a customer of mine who I happened to get away from just in time.

According to the news report, he was brought into this country by the very same uncle that he had killed. His uncle was a prominent business owner who had received awards for his business practices. He was brought to America to escape some very harsh conditions that he was living under in Korea. His uncle wasn't bringing him into poverty. He brought him into the land of opportunity where he had grown a business for himself and managed to live decently in a suburb outside of the city of Philadelphia. Now I'm not sure if Jo's cousin was the son of his uncle, but he too was a successful business owner who owned a cellphone store in North Philadelphia where I met them.

Maybe it's the years of weed smoke that won't allow me to remember why I chose this store in the first place, but I do remember very clearly being in the store and the energy attached to it. I was asking about the prepaid phones and made it very clear that I wanted a phone that did not require my name and address. In North Philly it was pretty obvious what I was looking for and why I was looking for it. I needed a phone to hustle from for those of you who haven't caught on. Jo's cousin seemed to understand, and we left the obvious unsaid, while Jo was all too eager to find out what I was really into. The two were very different people. One looked like an owner of a cellphone store. The other had a bunch of street tattoos, a gold chain, and was desperately trying to fit in with people that couldn't imagine owning a cellphone store.

After speaking about the phones, I told them I would stop back in, but Jo wasn't going to let me leave without blatantly asking me what I do. I cryptically told him that I make things happen. He pressed the issue despite the look on his cousin's face that I immediately picked up on. To me it was more than blurting out what I do to people in an establishment that I don't know, while having at least twenty pounds of weed at my residence. It was also about discussing illegal activity in front of the store owner who was going to sell me the phone to do it, and possibly jeopardizing his business. That look on his cousin's face forced Jo around the counter, where he then followed me out of the store. Well, now we're on the street and he wants to know what I do. Well, this is where I'll tell you. He then told me he could sell weed and needed my number. All I was thinking about at the time were the numerous shaky consignment arrangements that I had with people and finally here is a store owner for a customer. I shouldn't have any headaches.

At this point in my career I was only interested in selling the full pound, not half, not a quarter, just the whole thing. On my first phone call from him I broke my rule when he asked for a quarter pound. I told him I don't sell those and he began haggling. This was my first red flag. I didn't need this shit, and that is a feeling that he should have prevented. I decided to meet with him anyway and we met in the parking lot of his cousin's store. This is where he told me it was his cousin's store and expressed that he was upset we couldn't make this transaction in the store. Yea this guy was young and dumb! We met several more times for half pounds and quarters and almost every time he was five or ten dollars short, a disgusting habit. He would call with the utmost sense of urgency and would never have the full amount.

Throughout my dealings with him he would meet me driving a late model Jaguar, that was very nice and very new. I had purchased a new truck loaded with tv's and way too much space for one person, but that's what I wanted. I met Jo one day and jumped into the passenger seat of his Jaguar when he started going on and on about my new truck. I told him the truck is nice, but it's definitely not this car that you have. He told me the car was his cousin's and was mumbling something to the effect of his cousin being an asshole, and then of course, he was short again. Now I'm positive my business with this guy is over. Here I was thinking that I was dealing with a business owner who was successful enough to be partners in a cellphone business and buy a nice car for himself, when I'm actually dealing with someone who doesn't own a thing, and doesn't respect what others own. Imagine that, driving around in someone else's car for weeks buying drugs in it and calling them an asshole.

I began evading his calls in an attempt to disappear, sensing that business with him was going to lead somewhere I didn't want to be. When he called he had been labeled bullshit in my mind and there was no incentive to answering him. I eventually told him that I was looking for what he wanted and didn't have it at the time. I didn't know how much at the time, but I knew people like him were dangerous. About a month after dealing with him I saw him on every news channel, charged with the third degree murder of his uncle who he believed had a hundred thousand in cash in his home. When I heard the story unfold on the news I thought to myself, it sounds like him. What hit even closer to home was hearing that one of his codefendants lived on the very same street I did just over a block away. I couldn't help but think what someone petty enough to set up their own uncle would try to do to their weed man.

Lessons from story

Lesson One:
Don't Ignore Red Flags

All businesses have parameters. When you construct your business make sure you establish guidelines. Coloring outside the lines will lead you to where you don't want to be. The customer is always right mentality can destroy what you are trying to build. How can the customer always be right? Their goal is to get something from you for the lowest possible price, regardless of whether your business fails or not. This cliche will allow your customers too much freedom to roam into the back offices of your business and disturb your finances. Don't ignore the red flags of those who are overstepping the confines of being a customer. Businesses do survive off of customers, but when a customer starts to become something other than that, a problem ensues and they have to be treated accordingly. Remember the goal is not to make the customer happy, it's to make the customer satisfied. If you can agree that when you set up certain boundaries for your business's operations that you were of sound mind, then you should know that they are there for a reason and that compromising them is a risk that you will have to deal with the outcome of. For me, the red flag has been a matter of life and death.

Lesson Two:
Business That Doesn't Feel Good, Doesn't Pay Well Either

There is an extreme connection in business between feeling good and having financial gain. When business is done correctly it feels good. It feels much better to know the person you are dealing with has good business practices also. I've made plenty of transactions in undesirable places. There is a much greater comfort in knowing that you don't have to count the money in these places because the person you are dealing with has a reputation for doing honorable business. When you know that someone is going to be constantly complaining in an attempt to lower the price, or is short on the money, it doesn't feel good and makes you hesitate to answer their calls. These are the people that get weeded out when a company is forced to make changes. They are the first on list to go. This is how a customer gets fired because his services are no longer required. When you remain on the mind of a connect after he is finished working for the day, you are in dangerous waters. It means that he is uncomfortable with something that you are doing. This is not the machine like qualities they are looking for. Would you spend all night thinking about your refrigerator? You might if it wasn't functioning properly.

Lesson Three:
Petty Equals Dangerous

The petty minded individual should never be allowed to see too much. How much is too much? Anything is too much when it comes to the petty mind. When you are being shorted small amounts of money, it all adds up. You must constantly remind yourself that these calculated actions are the small signs that indicate that someone is trying to leverage your business. In the petty mind, you can take the loss. It's not their concern how you take it, they just assume that you can. It's all a matter of what they decide you can take. It might be five or ten dollars or maybe five hundred on a larger scale, but in the end someone else is deciding the fate of your money. They often choose to insert the "petty twist". The petty twist is when someone shorts you a small amount of money and if you ask for it you are now deemed petty for asking for such a small amount of money. You are now involved in a twisted petty ordeal over your own money.

The large scale petty twist is far more dangerous and stems from the first form of this petty nonsense. It's when someone has initiated several unaddressed petty twist on you, and is now envious of your ability to move on without the payments. They are now going to become a great story-teller, and tell you a greatly detailed fairytale about where your money has gone now that they've chosen to short you such a large amount. The petty mind is not one to play with. It is best when you see these types of behaviors to move on quickly. It's not worth your time or energy. Why reduce all of your great business ideas and ambitions of success by dealing with petty minded individuals?

The Bottom Line

The choice is yours between best friend or worst enemy when dealing with consignment. If you're being consigned, it comes down to recognizing your own need for being consigned, and taking into account what it is the person consigning you needs from you. On the opposing side, if you are consigning someone you have to be in search of machine like qualities that will allow you to sleep at night and operate without worries and concerns. Addressing the concerns of your connect will often lead to them giving you more than what you're asking for in order to see you less often. It means they now feel good about not seeing you everyday. You are becoming reliable and trustworthy, forcing a heavier consignment. Forced consignment equals a partnership. It's almost a favor to your connect that will ensure that you stay connected and when you're connected your customers are supplied, and that's business!

Chapter Four:
Quality Control: Sanford vs Jefferson

Finally, its time to start discussing product. My plan is not to tell you that you have to have the best product in order to be successful. That would be a load of bullshit, and even that would eventually sell. This is about being honest about how different qualities work in the marketplace. I don't expect you to believe that dollar stores can't prosper because they're selling inferior products. The product simply has to suit the customer's wants or needs. Making sure that you maintain the right product for your customer at all times is known as Quality Control. There are several different dynamics of how the quality of your product can impact your business. This is why controlling that quality is of so much importance.

In business, the goal is to make money while satisfying your customer. Don't confuse satisfaction with overcompensation. Your customer should feel confident in making transactions with you. This confidence comes from understanding what they are buying from you. This is why the average person hates to purchase a used car. Most people feel that if the car is in great shape or poor shape, the car salesman is going to use the same tactics and the same speech. This adds convolution into the picture, and makes it hard for the customer to understand the product, creating an unpleasant shopping experience.

If you study your business's environment correctly, you will be able to build a relationship with your customer predicated on honesty, which holds a great deal of value in the marketplace. What type of customer are you seeking? Does that customer even exist where your store is located? Are you providing what the people need, or what they want? These are questions that you have to be able to quickly answer to help you understand what you are providing, so that you can help your customer to understand that fact as well. No business can exist without sales. It is the heartbeat of any operation. Your heart rate can speed up, remain at a normal pace, or even slow down to a crawl, but it has to beat. Without that there is nothing to talk about, besides jump starting the heart to bring life back to the business.

In this chapter we're going to look intensely at different qualities of product, and how the existence of specific variables can effect the sale of them. We will explore everything from junk to premium, and examine the pros and cons of each of them. This will help to prevent you from sending mixed signals to your customer. At the end of the day there are two polar opposites to the word hustler. One end of the word is revered, and held in high esteem. It's associated with the great qualities of a self motivated salesperson. The other end of the word carries a very negative connotation that is normally generated by someone who has been hustled. My aim is to arm you with the information you need so that you can apply the proper etiquette to maintain your business's integrity.

Branding

Let's begin by discussing different types of quality, so that we can adequately speak on how to control it. I think most people would love to assume that they have a great product. At the very least, most people want their customers to feel that they are getting a great product. This introduces the concept of branding. There are several meanings attached to the word branding that may apply to this conversation. Let's look at the definitions and discuss them further.

Brand: noun
1. A type of product manufactured by a particular company under a particular name
2. An identifying mark burned onto livestock, criminals, or slaves

When examining the first definition of the word brand, we find that it alludes to a kind, or make of a product by a specific seller. It may be no different from what others are offering, just simply packaged and branded with the sellers name. It doesn't matter if the product is dog shit. I'm selling "Jus One's" brand of dog shit, which will be much more appealing than regular dog shit. We will learn how to effectively market products in the next chapter. Marketing and branding are two similar concepts, but very separate things.

I think the best example of branding in this aspect of the word, is what the Band-Aid brand of bandages has managed to achieve. They've made their brand synonymous with the actual product. This is an incredible feat to have accomplished, exemplifying what it means to create a brand. They've replaced the word bandage with the name of their product in the minds of patrons worldwide. Many people aren't aware that Band-Aid is the name of the brand and not the product. They get hurt and request a "Band-Aid".

The second definition of the word brand is the definition that will be most applicable in this discussion. You might be wondering how a mark burned into livestock or a criminal applies, but it will be your business's impression that is burned into the minds of everyone who encounters it. This will occur no matter if your business is good or bad, branding is happening. That's right, whether you realize it or not, your business is speaking for you. It's telling people to either come back or forget they were ever there.

Branding also requires a balancing act. You have to be careful not to overdo things while trying to reach your customer. What's the difference between an arrogant store owner and an over polite store owner? The answer is nothing. Both people are not desirable to do business with. You have to be careful not to allow customers into the back of your store, figuratively, or literally. Having phone conversations about business in front of customers, letting them witness deliveries, and sharing personal problems with them, are all ways to stifle your business. You might as well bring them into your office, show them your bills, and take them home with you. You have now branded things into the minds of your customer that have nothing to do with business. They will be able to associate things that they shouldn't have seen with your business. Being polite is one thing, but having them in your business is another. Enforce boundaries in your store and in your brain as well. Be mindful of what you are branding into your customers' memory banks. Thoughts can be extremely hard to remove.

Confidence in your product gives you greater control over the way you are able to deal with your customer. Let's now begin by looking into the advantages of having a quality product. What is your customer looking for? Quality plays a big role in satisfying them. Some people are looking for a lack of quality to save money, while others may be looking to pay more for a premium product. When products are placed in the right environment, they will sell themselves. For instance, if you were in a dollar store you wouldn't expect the salesman to try and convince you how superior the product you are buying is compared to others. It is placed in the proper setting. If you attempted to sell a diamond ring from this very dollar store, the setting can diminish the value of the product greatly.

Quality

Selling quality products leads to the most honest way to deal in business. You don't have to sell the customer on the attributes of the product. Instead you merely have to point them out and let the product speak for itself. What I've learned when dealing with people, is that they will pay for what they want, and beg for what they need. We all want to have quality in our lives. It is the justification for setting prices higher and driving margins higher along with them. Here are a few pros of dealing with only high quality products.

1. **The Truth**: You don't have to exaggerate the truth pertaining to the product. People are receptive to these things when making purchases. Exaggerations equal lies when in the realm of a transaction. When dealing with quality, you can use specific selling points to captivate your customer. This will turn the product into a want, and people find money for the things they want.
2. **The Pedestal**: You will be able to create clear distinctions from your products and others by using the good characteristics of your product to place it on a pedestal. Your product will sit higher in the minds of your customers compared to products of others, based solely on truth. This gives the customer the feeling of having to buy the product. Not doing so would be cheating their-selves out of the quality that all people feel they deserve.

3. **Bragging Rights**: Nothing can be better for business than having a customer brag to others about the quality of your product. Here you have the best salesman in the world speaking on behalf of your business without pay. They are now convincing others that your product is worth bragging about, removing doubt from the customers mind and replacing it with an eagerness to buy.

Having quality products eliminates the over-sell of your product. You don't have to become a pushy salesperson who finds that harassing a patron is the fastest way to the sale. Instead, the products features will speak to the customer, making it their loss if they choose not to purchase. Simply put, quality creates wants. It lingers in the mind of the customer, playing off of the human instinct to want nice things for themselves. This can make your job a lot easier by branding a level of quality next to your name.

Adversely, you may find that high quality may be destroying your business. This is why they don't sell Bentleys in the ghetto. What purpose would it serve? I'm sure some idiot will scrape their money together and be more than happy to park it outside of the projects. However, this will not be enough to sustain your business. Having products that are too high in quality for the neighborhood creates a museum effect. This is where customers walk around your store gazing at products that are too expensive for them to want to even touch, and then ultimately end up walking out the door. They will warn friends not to go into your store to avoid the embarrassment attached to the atmosphere your business provides. You have become a museum curator, rather than the salesman that you set out to be. Let's look at some of the negatives that can come with selling quality so that you will be able to properly establish the type of business that you want.

1. **A League of your own**: Don't confuse a league of your own with the majors. A league of your own means just that, there will be no one there to play with you. While you may have that great quality product that is easy to talk about, you might find that there isn't anyone willing to listen.
2. **A high quality insult**: Nobody likes to be reminded of how much they can't afford. It will cause them to avoid your business all together. There is a difference between having a good quality product, and having a product that offends people. What's the point? Place things in their proper setting to ensure that they are sold and not merely displayed.
3. **High prices Low profits**: When dealing with high prices, the place you buy from has the ability to sell you on the very same points you will use on your customer. You may find that quality is shrinking your margins and is now working against you by taking longer to sell and yielding less profits.

Real Life Application of Great Quality: The Rocafella Rolodex

In the early part of this new millennium my partners and I attempted to launch my rap career. I had built a corner that was at the time at its most successful point. My partner introduced to me a product that literally exploded my corner and eventually left an impact on the East Coast. At the time, we knew that we had the best weed in our neighborhood, and quickly learned it was some of the best in the country. Our corner was now a status symbol.

People felt that they were cheating themselves if they were paying for a product other than ours.

One day in the studio where I had booked a few hours to record, that weed in my pocket changed my life. I would always take a piece to share with my producer while recording. In one of our sessions he got a phone call from a local rapper by the name of Philadelphia Freeway. My producer reluctantly asked me if I would mind switching my time slot with Freeway. He expressed that he would understand if I didn't want to and would respect my decision because I was a paying customer. I had no problem telling him to take the session and switch my spot. This was a wise decision on my behalf. I left the studio and returned to the block to get back to business.

Almost immediately after returning to the block my phone rang. My producer told me to come back to the studio with more of what I had given him. Apparently Freeway was in the sharing mood also, and had shared some of his weed with the producer also. The producer's response was that it was good, but had nothing on what the guy who just left here had. Freeway told him to tell the guy to come back which prompted my phone to ring. His hit record "Roc the mic" was literally playing on the radio as I drove back to the studio, and all I could think of was one day recording with him. I came back into the studio with a pocket full of potency. Free bought all of it and took my number. I had no idea how long it would be before hearing from him again, but it turned out that it only lasted him about forty-eight hours before he was calling again. It was now time for him to come to the block to grab it. I could have delivered it to him but I thought it would be best for him to see with his own eyes what I was rapping about. I had planned to ask him to record with me on the third or fourth time meeting with me, yet when he came to the block for the first time he said these words before leaving,

"I got 16 for you. Early!" For those of you who don't know what that means, he offered to do a song with me.

"Was that Freeway who just came out of your spot?!?!" I was asked by one of my customers. I smiled and nodded my head and watched business erupt and reach new heights. People felt honored to be buying their weed from the same place as celebrities. They knew it was the best that they could get their hands on, but knowing it was the best he could put his hands on, changed everything. The quality spoke for itself. The price matched the quality making it hard for everyone to buy, but people will find ways to get what they want.

I wasted no time calling the producer who was charging me a thousand dollars a song. He said forget the money, let's get it done, and I agreed. He knew that it wasn't the time to worry about money because a song with Freeway would go much further than a thousand dollars. This time I brought my partner along and he and Free exchanged numbers. It made more sense this way because I was on the block and my partner couldn't sit still. It wasn't long before Freeway's industry friends got tired of him having the best weed around before he asked if they too could purchase from us. Now The Young Gunnz were added into the Rolodex. Beanie Siegel and Memphis Bleek soon followed. Our weed took us places that we couldn't have gone without it. When we sold it people looked. This helped us to develop our own level of celebrity. It just wasn't the type we were looking for. On one evening my partner had millions of record sales standing in his living room looking for something to smoke. It's too bad that Jay Z didn't smoke! Despite developing a list of celebrity clients that included Rocafella records, a local radio station, music producers, actors and more, we also engaged every successful cocaine and crack dealer in the neighborhood, we were amazed that this product wasn't available anywhere else.

The most memorable moment was one day when one of Jay Z's proteges asked if he could be met on the New Jersey Turnpike, and made a transaction before reaching the toll booth on the side of the road. This was some stink shit to make a celebrity drive from out of state to buy weed on the side of the highway. This particular product opened doors that had security codes on them. We didn't have to "sell" it. We just had to sell it. My crew and I walked through the doors of Baseline Studios, Rocafella headquarters, due to the quality of our product. I can vividly remember watching Jay Z record "Welcome to New York" featuring Cam'ron, while knowing what brought us into the building. When reminiscing on this time, two thoughts fill my head. The first is, if you've got beef with Free, you've got beef with me! I know that he didn't have to be as generous as he was. My second thought is that it's a damn shame that Jay Z didn't smoke!

Lessons from story

Lesson One:
The Power Of A Sample

When dealing with quality, the sample can yield great rewards. It's a matter of who you decide to share your product with. The discretion is what will make your sample grow legs or grow roots. Your sample can go much further than you can, but you can't allow your product to be abused. Quality is its own advertisement. When you place it in the right hands you give it a far greater potential. It comes down to the type of person you are giving it to, and for what reason. Giving it to a hustler is much different then giving it to a customer. Hustlers have to have the accessibility to make their customers aware of their new product. Customers have to understand that after being privy to the products quality, samples are for pulling in mass amounts of new customers, not to entice an existing one. Be mindful that there are customers who can transform into hustlers when given the opportunity to present a great product for someone else. Spotting these types of customers can also expand your business.

Lesson Two:
No One Wants To Be Left Out

The quality product is contagious. It exudes an aura of higher status that plays heavily on the mind of consumers. People feel the need to obtain quality. Even when it is not a wise financial decision, it remains in the mind of the consumer. It will at times fester to the point of being addressed by consumption. This is what you want as a hustler, products of desire. Quality products are closely related to human desire. People are not walking around thinking about one day obtaining a subpar product. That would be against human nature. Feeling that others deserve things that you don't isn't a thought of a rational mind. No one wants to be left out, when it comes down to a good Quality of Life!

Lesson Three:
Quality Opens Bigger Doors:

Having product alone is a great door opener in life. It gives you a reason to go places the average person cannot go. It also opens conversation to you that may not have been extended to you had you not had something to offer. The people you meet, and doors that you walk through can be a result of having products. With that being said, the greater the product, the greater the doors you will be able to walk through. In my life, I've sold some high quality products as well as low quality ones. The most significant doors in my life to open for me were a direct result of having premium quality. It actually had the people inside those doors saying, "He's one of us". It takes you greater places and gives the implication that you are supposed to be there, because you are. Weed has opened a lot of doors for me, but the kind of weed celebrities wanted, unlocked the studio door, and those experiences are priceless.

When dealing with hustling, it is important to always explore both sides of the spectrum. We've seen examples how having good quality products can work for you, and in some cases work against you. This is the same truth that surrounds products of lesser quality. It is about how you apply these truths, and when you apply these truths in our current situations. Knowing what you have and what it's worth will help to give you the right mindset to achieve success in your business. Now let's dive right into the dumps and find the diamond among it.

The Lack of Quality

First off, I want to throw away the notion that having a quality product is the only way to make money. That is the type of bullshit that will have you thinking that dollar stores can't make money and fancy antique shops can. There is a balance that must exist in all businesses. This comes from knowing your customers, your location, and what you have to offer. What I've come to realize is that everything will sell. It's just a matter of who needs it and how accessible it is to them. Have you ever noticed that malls with expensive items can sell cheap food? Your customers' actions speak loudly and clearly. Make sure that you listen when they speak. It's the difference between a drug dealer and a drug pusher. Pushing things on people will not last as long as being a dealer, and products of lesser quality require pushing.

Sometimes people are looking for something cheap. The mother who wants to simply hang a picture on the wall isn't looking for a quality hammer, with a comfortable leather handle to put her nails in the wall. She is looking for a product of convenience. You may be looking for a sophisticated customer to patronize your establishment, and in reality get an average Joe buying from your shop. You won't know your customer until you start selling. Then and only then will you know if your products are right for your customer. Let's now take a look at the pros of putting lesser quality products into the marketplace.

1. **Cost effective**: While quality products have their virtues, lesser quality products that are more affordable can sell much faster. Saving a dollar is always a great selling point in any realm of business. It just comes down to what are they saving on, and will the product get the job done. Being able to appeal to your customer's pocket is a great way to fill your own.
2. **More sales**: You may find that your business is positioned to make ten $10 sales before it will make one $100 sale. That is the same hundred dollars, without the fight. Lower priced products attract more people than higher priced ones in certain atmospheres. This creates the opportunity to make more transactions, giving a business more traffic to eventually exploit.
3. **No selling required**: While the same extreme exist within quality products, extremely lesser quality products can also require little to no selling. The quality speaks for itself. When priced accordingly, people will not require these things to be pushed onto them. It is quite clear what they are buying and to be sold on its

attributes would be being lied to. It's simply not necessary to do so. This is what makes things confusing to the customer and results in no sales.

Making money while selling products of lower cost can actually be a rewarding experience. It is a situation where everyone involved is satisfied and that's the key to business, satisfying your customer. The less convolution, the better, as long as things are clear to your customer when business is transpiring. When the lines are confusing regarding what your customer is paying for, a swindle is occurring, because it is your job to make the customer aware of the truth. In business, that's what matters the most. Remember there's nothing wrong with selling bullshit, as long as you're not disguising it as quality.

Without question, we know that there are undoubtedly a few cons in the realm of dealing with lesser quality. It should be obvious that the very same pros of having quality, would expose the negatives of having lesser qualities. Let's look a little closer at the negative outcomes that can come from dealing with these inferior products.

1. **Nothing Special**: when there is nothing special about a product it has very little desirability. There is nothing compelling anyone to buy it other than need, and a need can also compel someone to search for a quality item. It also makes for pushy conversations, trying to drive a sale in your direction. The conversation has little to do with the product because the price is the major selling point.
2. **Too much room to negotiate**: the lower the quality, the taller the customer. Customers who contemplate quality also contemplate pricing. It gives them leverage when it comes to negotiations, and too much leverage in the hands of a customer is a threat to your business. Products that are too low in quality are at risk of not

being sold, and customers can pick up on this. It's their job to spot ways to drive down costs in their favor.

3. **Negative Branding**: When people label your business with the stamp of poor quality, it isn't an easy one to remove. It has been found in business that negative news travels much faster than positive news does. This can be detrimental when dealing with a negative label on your business. The burden is not on the public to restore faith in your business. This takes undoing, and in business undoing is never as easy as doing.

Real Life Application of Poor Quality: Shit Made Things Shittier

Beware, the title of this story speaks for itself and actually sums up a pretty shitty story. There have been times in my years of hustling when I was forced into dealing with subpar products, low grade weed to be exact. To be perfectly clear I've made plenty of money selling bullshit weed when there was no other option. Obtaining it for cheap and selling it for just under market value has made me a lot of profit. What isn't often talked about is the negative branding associated with doing this, and how after time passes you will be left with a label that you will try desperately to remove.

An older friend of mine who had been selling weed for most of my life would become the biggest example of this negative branding that I could share. He specialized in selling low grade weed in bulk. If you needed pounds of weed, this was your man. He had no problem dumping pounds of weed on me to make it disappear like a drug dealing magician. He had a philosophy that everything would sell, and he was right. Drugs in America will always find their way to a customer. There is no such thing as a drug that won't sell. However, there is such a thing as boomerang drugs. These boomerang drugs are drugs that leave your door, appear to be gone, and return later that evening, next day, or possibly even days later. In the street this is an extreme red flag. It creates more driving of an illegal product, free of charge. When the product is returned no one makes money. It becomes a loss due to wasting gas and time.

My friend was selling this low quality bud for so long that the standard on the street had changed several times, while the quality of his product remained the same. He had gone from a go-to player to someone who sits on the bench. Word began to travel that it would be a waste of your time if you purchased from him. If your customer didn't choose to return the product, they will become hesitant to buy from you again. In desperate situations I would find myself traveling across the city to look at his junk and debate whether it would become a boomerang. I began noticing that after dealing with him my customers would always call back and say, "Let me know when things change". This meant that I was falling victim to negative branding. The more I would pass off my friend's product, the more my reliability was brought into question. This is when I realized that my attempts to fill voids and gaps in my business by selling my friend's trash were damaging my reputation, forcing me into a serious reconstruction phase. My friend's business was eventually reduced to being patronized only when better quality couldn't be found. He was and still is negatively branded in the game.

Lessons from the story

Lesson One:
Throw Darts Not Boomerangs

Selling things that will return is a waste of time! It creates a loss on behalf of both parties. People are now paying to work, rather than working to get paid. While it is a good practice to accept the return, these returns send bad signals to customers. It confirms their doubt, when their customers refuse the product. It doesn't comply with the rules of satisfaction. The product eventually has to sell for much cheaper than originally priced, and in some cases sells to someone who was offered a higher price for the product previously. This is what happens when you don't put a bullshit price on bullshit, it becomes a boomerang. It's better to be straight forward and throw darts. Your customers will respect you more for being direct.

Lesson Two:
Disappearing Acts Are For Magicians

All that disappears is not gone! What this means is that just because a product sells doesn't mean it can't damage your business. People often think because a product has been sold that it means their customer is satisfied, and if not satisfied, they'll get over it. Just because a product has disappeared, doesn't mean that your credibility isn't being destroyed in the process. One of the worst scenarios to be in is having a customer constantly in search of a new connect. This simply means that your product has them dissatisfied and now questions your judgement as well as your moral compass. Properly pricing it, and calling it what it is, are helpful ways to get rid of the shit, but it is negative brand association. Even though you're being honest about the poor quality, the quality will still be associated with your brand.

Lesson Three:
Last On The List

Out of all the creatures in the ocean to be, you've become a bottom feeder. This is what being last on the list entails. It means being thought of when all else fails, or when serving a customer you don't mind losing. It means your business now relies on the failure of another business, or customers who can't afford to go anywhere else. These are often undesirable customers that cause confusion because of the pettiness attached to such poor quality products. Being last on the list means competing with no sale at all. Doing business with a bottom feeder becomes a risk for anyone above them on the food chain. They have already been branded and that brand association will bring negative attention to your business.

Bottom Line

The bottom line is that you must know your customer's needs and how they relate to what you have to offer. Maintaining the quality your customers require is a full time job. Be aware that a customer that buys without returning can be a result of negative branding, or possibly lead to negative branding. Master your environment so that you know what you are providing. Don't try to bring quality where it can't benefit you, nor bring junk to the high end district. This is a balancing act that you must learn to accomplish.

Chapter Five:
Marketing Madness:
Water for Whales

Welcome to the wide world of marketing! You have now entered the ever expanding universe of moving product. Enjoy the guided tour as the secrets to this universe begin to unfold before you, and don't forget to buckle up. Now let's begin. The first stop on our journey is in the galaxy of reality. Here is where I will explain to you how you've just been pulled in by a marketing ploy to make everything bigger. This is what marketing is all about. It's about creating a smoother ride. This paragraph's opening sentences were designed to pull you into my world. I could have easily opened by stating that this was a chapter on marketing and began discussing that topic. Instead, I chose to speak about the universe, and planet, buckling up a seatbelt, and taking a tour of the galaxy. This was a much more exciting approach to opening this chapter.

In actuality the opening sentences do fit this chapter very well. The concept of marketing is as big as the universe, and you have to think as big as the universe to do so. This is where the phrase think outside of the box comes into play. You must destroy the box that your mind is trapped in so that you can destroy the box that is trapping your customer's minds as well. What you must understand is that marketing exists in everything. It ranges from the clothes we wear to the words we choose. Once you really understand that fact, marketing will begin to become an easier task.

Always keep and open mind when developing a marketing strategy. This will help you to choose the angle from which you will approach your project. There is one main point that we will explore in parts when it comes to marketing, and that is perception. This is the driving force behind your five senses. Seeing, hearing, tasting, touching, and smelling all come back to perception. Marketing is creating perception, perception of a product or of a brand. Let's take a look at the two different aspects of marketing. It is not necessary to separate good quality vs poor quality when speaking about marketing. Marketing is about creating a perception, and the same effort should be given to doing so regardless of the products quality.

Marketing a product: When you market a product, there are several components to look at. I've split them into two parts that I call Greater Greats and Intentional Flaws. First, we will begin by examining how to produce Greater Greats.

Greater Greats

There are many women who believe that when taking photographs they have a good side. The reality is that they do. There is one particular angle that looks better than the rest. Don't be lazy, search for it, and when you find it exploit it. Do your best to unlock your products potential. Your product has a date with your customer, make sure it has sex appeal. Buyers should be enticed to buy. If this wasn't the case, all packaging would be the same. It wouldn't matter how products were dressed up or talked about, if enticing buyers wasn't a must. The products we see were all designed to attract customers.

Some do a better job than others. This is very similar to preparing for a date. Some people do a better job than others in this area as well. If you are often complemented on your eyes, don't wear shades on your date. When marketing products, always take an artistic approach to displaying them.

Creating greater greats requires following through on your presentation. Having a great establishment equipped with all the bells and whistles is a great thing to have, but you have to follow through. Why have a beautiful establishment and then decide to make a subpar flyer to attract clients? You are creating a standard. Everything associated with your product should be calculated. Gaining a customer is the same as getting a yes for a date request. You want the customer to fall in love with the product and come back for a second date. The greater the great, the better chance you will have of seeing them again. Good conversation is a plus, and so is a great working product, but when reflecting on your date or the time you've spent staring at the product in a store, you will always remember sexy. Ask yourself, how often the food on the menu resembles what is brought to you on a plate? It's clear the menu is interested in displaying sex appeal to gain your attention.

Sex appeal in marketing is what has inspired my motto for maintaining it. "Everything and everyone needs a Logo". The logo is a push-up bra for your product. It gives you something to stare at, and something to stare at is something to remember. Logos are a requirement for any serious attempt at enticing customers. The consumer sees them as a stamp of approval, certifying the product. The funny thing about this is that you are in control of your own certification. Let's suppose I go to the park and scoop up some dirt and put it into several clear plastic packages and attempted to sell it. Now let's take that same package and put a sticker on it with a professional logo that says P.F.

Philadelphia's Finest soil. I have just transformed dirt from the park into an official looking soil from an established entity. Now this is just regular dirt. Think of the possibilities of how a professional logo can help you in your business.

I think that logos should be abused and not just used. They should be everywhere and on everything. Wouldn't your restaurant's bathroom door look a lot better with a logo for the word "men's", rather than having the same stick figure that you see everywhere? Start by ordering a personal logo for yourself. Take your first and last name or possibly just your initials and have it whipped into a logo. Use your logos on letterheads, resumes and more. Watch the reactions you receive from them as you turn yourself into a brand that should be taken seriously. You may already be a great person, but business is about making Greater Greats. The logo adds commitment, and creates a product. It can turn something as simple as a lemonade stand into a business. If you are a rapper, lawyer, barber, etc, have a logo made and attach it to your business card and you will be on your way to a second date.

When dealing with product, always take the time to greater the great. It may be the way you use lighting in a picture, or even cleaning the product thoroughly before displaying it. Always keep in mind the perception you are creating. Is five minutes of cleaning worth more to you than not having your product sell for months? If so, then subpar is the way to go for you. For me, I'm much more interested in making great things greater, and not so great things great. Remember these products are just like life. It all depends on how you look at it!

Intentional Flaws:

What is an intentional flaw? It sounds like purposely adding flaws to a product. If that were the case you should close this book and hand it to your worst enemy because that is the only way it would do you any good. What intentional flaws are really about is creating an aura around your product that says even the flaws are supposed to be there. This a great selling tool that is often overlooked. It requires using reverse psychology to gain the attention of your customer. An intentional flaw in the same dating analogy would be a flaw that your date found cute and you finding opportune times to flaunt it. It may be a laugh, a sneeze or some sort of quirk that you are unable to avoid. We all have these flaws and in the right situations even a flaw can be exploited. Products are very similar. Sometimes the flaw can become a selling point.

Intentional flaws is about changing the perception of the flaw. It can be done in a serious way or jokingly, but if done correctly the result will equal more sales. Let's look at a few examples so you can fully understand this concept. Let's use junk food in our example. When it comes to food, junk food is considered to be flawed. Now let's take the flaw and accentuate it in our ad. We'll start off by taking this junk food and placing it on a silver platter in a fine dining setting. Let's have a fully uniformed butler pouring soda into a champagne glass. Now the only thing in this picture that is flawed is the actual product, but you are playing several tricks on the mind by creating this intentional flaw. Although there is an extreme contrast, your flawed product is being associated with the finer things. It doesn't matter if it is jokingly or not. The visual has been planted. This is one way to present an intentional flaw. It's about not hiding the problem.

Another example of this principle is to explain the flaw in succession with the products great attributes, adding the flaw in as if it were one of the items features. Don't hide it, talk about it with the same confidence you have when speaking on the good features of the product. Treat it like an intentional flaw. There are some people who don't mind having products that have the occasional flaw, and there are others that didn't know that it was ok for them to not mind the occasional flaw. They present false feelings of everything having to be perfect, and are amazed to find a sales person speak on a flaw so confidently, making it ok.

Using intentional flaws is very much about knowing your customer and implementing the right timing. They can be insulting to some people who are simply willing to pay to have the best quality product they can find. The intentional flaw will not serve you well in this instance. It could very well strip you of the credibility needed to sell to high end customers. Make sure that when using this tactic you are not aiming it at someone who is willing to pay top dollar. This is not for those types of individuals. Intentional flaws are for people who are actually concerned about the dollars they spend. It gives them an honest alternative to overreaching their spending. When used correctly people will appreciate the intentional flaw for allowing them to feel better about purchasing a somewhat inferior product. Stripping customers of pride may get you a sale or two, but it won't bring you reoccurring customers. Who plans to continuously have their pride stolen from them? People want to feel good about their purchases, no matter how big or small. If it doesn't feel good, the body isn't going to allow it to keep happening. It will begin to reject it. Take the time to discover your product's flaws and change the perception of them by subtly accentuating them. Who knows we may very well see fine dining McDonald's in the future, once they understand the principle of the intentional flaw.

Packaging is Everything

Don't judge a book by its cover! This has to be one of the dumbest statements in business. It sounds good, but has very little application in the real world. Asking people not to judge something by its appearance is absurd. It doesn't mean that they have to act as if they've reached a definitive conclusion to the books contents. However, they are allowed to judge if it will be of interest to them by simply looking at the cover. It's natural to look at the appearance of something and form judgements about it. Whether it's a person, movie, or a book, the cover or packaging is extremely important. Think about it in these terms. If you were trying to decide between the music of two of your favorite artists, don't you think the cover might have something to do with your decision? The cover and packaging is art, and art is a part of consumerism. Don't fool yourself into believing in silly cliches like "don't judge a book by its cover" or "its what's inside that counts". This is complete bullshit in the realm of business. If you lay these products on the floor even a baby will choose according to what is attractive to them. It's human nature.

Think about how your product is packaged or displayed for a significant amount of time. In the same vein you should also take into consideration how you are personally packaged and displayed. Do you look believable? Are you being displayed to the world in the best way possible? When given the option would you choose someone else over you strictly based off of appearance? You must answer these questions openly and honestly before making your product one of choice. You don't have to bullshit people by hiding flaws and embellishing truths to succeed. Make sure your product is properly dressed before it enters the beauty contest known as the stores shelf.

Marketing a Brand: The marketing of a brand is not very different from the marketing of a product. I've also broken the marketing of a brand into two parts as well. These parts have been coined, the experience and the lifestyle. Let's begin by looking at what is required of you to create the experience.

Selling An Experience

Intangible items and services are the elements of selling an experience. Nobody wants a bad experience. Experience relies on the exchange when you enter an establishment. It might be the conversation or even the lack of conversation that is pertinent to your customer. Knowing what type of experience your customer is looking for will help you to provide a better one. You may be attracted to the speed of a Little Caesar's pizza place, where you can buy a pizza in about 30 seconds, or maybe it's the great conversation at a local mom and pop style pizza shop that will garner your attention. The two are very different but they are both selling an experience, and anything being sold can be marketed.

Possibly you've had a good experience with a lawyer, separate from winning a case. It might've been the way they quickly returned phone calls or sent you text message updates. Now you are selling an experience. Don't make the mistake of thinking your tangible item is the only thing being sold in your transaction. The experience of purchasing is equally a part of this transaction and does hold value. That it what is made tangible when in the context of marketing. This isn't as much about knowing your customer as much as it is about knowing yourself. For example, the slogan "The friendliest place in town" shouldn't be used for an establishment where the owner doesn't like to talk much. That wouldn't be the right angle to approach that particular place. Focus on your strengths, speed, efficiency, whatever it is, play off of it, and it will create a marketing strategy based on truth.

The truth is the most pertinent aspect of your marketing strategy. Without it, you will be branded as a liar and that's worse than not being the best at what you do. When you create slogans you are creating expectations. If the expectations are not entertained, then you have been branded as a bullshitter. What this means is calling yourself the fastest delivery service in town without even attempting to show your customer that it might actually be true, leads to the worst type of business. This business is referred to as bullshit, because you have chosen to go against what your company stands for in the eyes of the public. The deception on behalf of the business will result it being negatively branded. Remember, that falls in line with the negative connotations associated with the word hustler, and those stigmas can be extremely hard to remove or replace.

The slogan is a very useful tool for someone trying to market an experience. The beauty of creating a slogan is it is you creating your own standard. You won't have to live up to the expectations of others. You will be competing with the bar that you've set in place. If your fries are average that won't stop you from advertising the worlds best burger. It doesn't compromise your integrity like it would if you would have said that you had the best fries. In business you're going to have to live up to some standard. The slogan allows the focus to be drawn towards your strengths as opposed to areas where your customer would like for you to be strong. It allows you to prepare them for the experience you intended for them to have. This is an easy way of creating something tangible from the intangible, and this is the key to marketing an experience.

Experiences can become products in the world of business. You might be told that you could receive a better haircut at another barbershop, but are satisfied with the experience you receive by your current barber. It's important that you materialize your intangible products when marketing your business. Take the time to test the slogans of a business and see how they compare to what they are offering. When it comes to your business remember that all of your actions are apart of the branding process, not just the transaction.

Selling A Lifestyle

Lifestyle businesses require the most amount of marketing efforts. Examples of lifestyle business are musicians, artist, personal training, etc. They are businesses that depend upon buying into a lifestyle. When you buy art, music, or select a personal trainer you have bought into a lifestyle. Marketing a lifestyle is an extremely targeted form of marketing. You have to be willing to exclude large demographics of people in exchange for targeting another. Lifestyles are sold every day. It's the unspoken part of a marketing ploy that we see all the time. The reason why you may not recognize this is because of its exclusionary nature. Often what happens is it is ignored by the people it is not intended for.

We've all seen many different examples of insurance companies. They all do the same thing, pay out claims on your policy. Yet there are many different classes of companies to support the many lifestyles of its customers. People who have achieved certain levels of security in their lives are willing to pay for their choices. They are not interested in paying less because the product doesn't match their lifestyle. Reversing this scenario will prove that people with a lesser income will buy outside of their lifestyle when dealing with tangibles, and not so much when it comes to intangible products. They are not so much concerned with having a premium phone company or having the best car insurance. They are lifestyle brands that can't be displayed, only enjoyed by the patrons of them.

Selling lifestyles doesn't at all mean that you have to focus on higher quality, but the focus will be on quality. There are different extremes when it comes to brands. You might want to build off of a niche, or you may adversely like to celebrate the fact that your product is for everyone. When selling a lifestyle you are saying that you are aware of the many products on the market but yours is for THIS type of person and THESE kinds of people. It doesn't ignore that other demographics exist, while creating validity for itself.

Lifestyle brands in some cases become closely aligned with scams when they attempt to provide premium quality for under the average costs. When this is done to intentionally mislead the customer to a negative outcome, it is a scam. This type of business is not what business is really about and will not be co-signed by me at any point in time, and will be later discussed in chapter nine, where we will explore morality in depth. When good intentions are involved, marketing higher quality lifestyles at affordable rates can be of great benefit. If you have the ability to provide what you are displaying, you will achieve extremely high profits in exchange for your services. When in the business of selling lifestyles, remember everyone is a potential client.

Don't Forget The Garnish!

I can't forget that day as a child when I went to a restaurant with my family and had stuffed my mouth full of garnish. I was told I didn't have to eat it and that it was just there to serve as dining decor to dress up the plate. It stuck with me how things were used to accent other things. It might be a lemon, lime, or cherry, but garnish shouldn't be limited to food. Garnish should be added to every marketing project that you encounter. It means adding something to dress up your product or scenario. Which situations or products require garnishing? All of them!

Garnish is the tissue paper in the shoebox, or the designer business card given after a meeting. It means that you have invested in your customer. It shows them that they are appreciated. You haven't just slapped their food on a dish and given it to them. You have taken pride in your presentation and added the right amount of garnish to earn the respect of your customer. It should be applied to every aspect of marketing.

In the end, garnish is a symbol of mutual respect between business owners and customers. It serves both parties equally. The customer feels the respect and reciprocates it back to the owner. Create visual and verbal forms of garnish to accentuate your business dealings, and watch as the respect of your customer helps to grow your enterprise. Envision your projects as a plate of food and remember, don't forget the garnish!

Water For Whales

In this section water for whales we will explore the world of advertising. The phrase selling water to a whale is the epitome of moving product, and that is what marketing is all about. I tend to look at the glass as half full. Whales do need water, so why not sell them some? Advertising wouldn't be the industry it is today if controlling your perception of products wasn't so important. Are you aware of the astonishing amounts of money paid for Super Bowl ads? It doesn't matter what business you are in, if you want it to scale, you're going to need advertising. Advertising requires every marketing tool you can muster to pull off the best work. There are two advertising styles that I'd like to take a look at, The Pioneer vs The "Everybody does it this way, now it's my turn to do it the same exact way" type of guy, who I refer to as Mr. Ditto. I'm sure the hustler in you can see where I'm going with this.

The Pioneer: When it comes to marketing, the pioneer is the one who has broadened his horizon by allowing their own creativity to expose them to customers who wouldn't have noticed them before. The pioneer doesn't blindly follow traditional methods of advertising without thought. He pushes the boundaries and creates templates rather than using them. The pioneer has the mentality of a true artist. He is not interested in painting pictures that have already been painted. His business is a work of art to be admired. Pay close attention to the moves of a pioneer, they may very well become your template.

Mr. Ditto: Mr. Ditto makes no deviations. All of his ideas are not even worthy of being called ideas. It is just the resurgence of something that has been done numerous times before. He doesn't have a creative bone in his body and is fearful of those that do. Mr. Ditto uses the same templates that everyone in his field have used previously. It may be the exact same menu template, or the same color scheme that is constantly repeated. He feels comfort in knowing that his business looks identical to the others in his field. It doesn't bother him because he is a follower, uninterested in forging new paths. This means his destiny doesn't belong to him, he is at the behest of those willing to drive his industry. When you become a follower in marketing you are bringing nothing new to the table, and that's exactly what your customers will get, nothing new!

We've established that marketing can be as big as your mind can imagine, and that everything is a part of marketing. Now we are going to look at the keys to maintaining this mentality.

It's Your Business, Be Unique!

Are you the owner or does the business own you? Many people look at their business through the scope of the baby metaphor. Using this same analogy, ask yourself this. Does your baby tell you the type of stroller to buy or what kind of clothes to purchase? Of course not! Your baby is in your hands, just as your business is. Would you try to dress your baby in the exact same outfits as the neighbors' kids? Probably not. This is the same as trying to emulate the business of someone else. How many pizza restaurants do we need with red and white walls? It may make the place feel more Italian but what is it doing in terms of differentiating itself from the rest. Did they not understand that if they were thinking outside of the box they might've ended up with the entire universe painted on the wall with the slogan "Best slices in the Galaxy" and a line of customers to prove it?

The best part of owning a business is having control of your destiny. There is no one in the way of you seeing your visions come to life. It's just a matter of your visions being creative enough. If you're not the creative type, keep creative minds close. Trust them to be as good at creating as you are at running your business, and be prepared to hug the block of course. If there is nothing unique about your business why expect above average sales? Since you are the owner the creative edge is something that you are required to provide. It's not a maybe or a plus, but rather a necessity. If nonexistent, you are to blame. Let me guess, in your next project you are opening a sneaker store where the employees will wear black and white striped shirts huh?

There's Always A New Way To Advertise!

Don't believe for one second that advertising stops at commercials and flyers. The methods you could employ are endless. Daring to be different is a must in marketing. Following cookie cutters, templates, and coloring in the lines is just as boring as it sounds. Where's all of the excitement in that? You have to find ways to excite the consumers by catching them off guard. Taking the same approach as everyone else is playing follow the leader instead of being a leader. Let's look at some ways of being different in the world of marketing. It can be as simple as not using flyers and using balloons instead. As long as you are creating a spectacle to gain attention, respectably of course.

Planning on airing a commercial? What's going to be different about it? How about enlisting a comedian instead of an average voice over? Maybe you can find a poet that will fit your businesses style. Again, there are endless tactics you could employ. It's best when they are thoughtful and have shock value. That doesn't mean you need fireworks it just means to use other angles besides what has been done already. No matter what it is you decide to do you should be confident that it's never been done in the way your doing it. The best way to achieve this is to take your time. Brilliant ideas sometimes come on a whim, but when planning, don't be lazy on the creative parts. Your business will suffer.

Be bold in your approach. You might want to push a few boundaries when seeking attention. Let's line every parking meter on the street with a balloon with an arrow on it pointing towards your business. Maybe we should have attractive woman with our logo body painted on them. Why don't we send ten pizzas to the local fire department, courtesy of our business that has nothing to do with pizza or firefighting. Let's be brave, and boldly go where no business has gone before!

Don't Spend, Create!

A little can go a long way. The growth of small businesses depends on being able to control your capital in the early stages of its growth. Advertising can become extremely costly for the uncreative. Nothing can bring out creativity as much as financial constraints. If a lack of finances can do this wonderful act for you, it is best to approach marketing as if you don't have much to spend. Take the clothing designer who doesn't have enough to purchase an ad in a magazine, but sent his shirts to the radio station for the DJ's to wear. What about having a talented but starving artist make a song for your business that you could shoot a video for, and advertise on YouTube or other social media sites. This can be pulled off for maybe a hundred dollars or less and can be extremely beneficial to your business. Maybe you own a flower shop and can't afford a radio ad. Why not send a few bouquets to local salons on a busy Saturday? These are the types of things that won't necessarily be on the front of your mind if you have the money to shoot a commercial, but may increase your chances of success just as much.

Cross promotion is a great tool for financially pressed entrepreneurs. Working with other business owners is a wise decision for growing your base. Find businesses that can exchange services and advertisements with you to save money while gaining customers. The biggest mistake in advertising is thinking that spending all of your budget on ads will lead to a guaranteed success. The only way to truly accomplish success is by winning over your customers. Buying your customers will not last. Eventually you will run out of money, or your customers will start to sneak off and seek out what they really want.

Only a fool doesn't use social media. The age of free advertisement has arrived. Here is where creativity is key. Engage people, throw contests, reward people for promoting your products. You have to merge the social media world with the real world, and then merge that world with your world. Your business is relying on you to be as creative as you can. Some of the greatest ideas in advertising were inspired by simply not having the funds to do anything otherwise.

Real Life Application Of Product Marketing: Hey Hey Hey!

At one point in my business rollercoaster ride I was in a rough situation. I was 23 years old and didn't think I had another block run in me. I had graduated to moving weight for some years and was bounced back to the block out of desperation. One thing I would always maintain in the street was A-1 credit. I could get a consignment at any time from anyone that knew me. At the time, good product was scarce and I didn't have an outlet for the small quantities that would be asked for on the block. My friend who lived around the corner insisted that we could turn his block into one of value.

We lived in the worst section of Philadelphia, in the heroine filled streets known as "The Badlands". The drug of choice was definitely not weed. That was almost laughed at by dealers, customers, and police alike. This provided a unique opportunity to move product without gaining the attention of the police. The problem was that we were selling garbage, and this would require some marketing. This was an uphill battle for several reasons. My partner lacked the experience in starting and maintaining a block. It was more than what was seen on television and rap videos, and at the end of the day the connect would be calling my phone for the payment.

We were off to a slow start that eventually grew into a small steady flow of traffic. One day my connect came through with the only thing he could find, a huge pound of brown bullshit weed. It was going to take forever to sell without some sort of ploy to gain attention. I looked at the sign on the street that read Albert street. I began thinking of Fat Albert who was also from North Philly. We had to stuff our bags with this brown weed until they were much fatter than the average dime bags. Selling them from Albert street in North Philly made me one day jokingly dub the product as "Fat Alberts". The joke actually began to gain traction when people started to refer to them as Fat Alberts also. I knew this wasn't going to last as a marketing strategy and that finding better product was a must, but it was a strong enough strategy to sell a pound of weed in dimes on a block with minimal traffic. Sometimes being creative is the only way to save yourself from starving.

Lessons from story

Lesson One:
It's Never Over

If you haven't waved the white flag it's not over. Business will always bring out the best in you. It requires you to think outside of the box to eventually think your way out of the box. When things aren't going your way you have to redirect the situations to make things flow in your direction. Being a hustler is being able to adapt to any business environment. Some people are only able to function in business when the situation is perfect. Their commitment or ability to resolve problems hasn't been tested. There is no way to know who will fold in times of adversity. Many people appear to be great at business in situations that haven't tested them. Your favorite boxer should not be someone who is afraid to fight. Throwing in the towel is not the way to winning over your fans. Your favorite fighter may have losses on their record, but having the heart to fight off of the ropes can prove them to be deserving of admiration. When in business make sure that you fight the good fight!

Lesson Two:
Give Them What They Want

We all know what our customers want. Maybe its quality, maybe its quantity, but we do know the answer. When one thing is lacking you have to compensate for it. You can't pretend that everything is fine and will be acceptable to your customers. Actually, you can pretend, but you can't expect your customer to pretend with you. Customers have an allegiance to satisfaction, not to their suppliers. Business is about profiting from providing what people want. They may eventually get tired of what you are providing, so it is your job to be creative when exploring the wants of your customer. If you're lacking quality, give them more. Be upfront about what it is they are getting and it will be more believable to them that it is something that they should want. Giving people what they want in business shouldn't be treated as a survival tactic. It should be seen as the only way to exist. Remember giving your customers what they want is the best way to get what you want, which isn't just money, it's also their respect that your after!

Lesson Three:
If Your Serious They'll Believe You

The poker face is often used, but not required. It is about keeping a straight face regardless of whether you are bluffing or not. The key in business is to not bluff. When you are upfront about the offers that you're presenting, the bluff and poker face are two unnecessary tools in your office. Creating serious offers will allow you to be genuine in your approach, and the customer will follow. They are aware of what they are purchasing or experiencing and will not feel hustled when making a transaction. If they do feel hustled, they will quickly realize that they have hustled themselves into believing in something other than what was presented to them. Sellers often list products and state the words "serious inquiries only". The same respect should be afforded to customers by being a serious seller. Customers want and need to feel sincerity. Remember, just because someone is wearing a poker face doesn't mean they aren't bluffing!

Real Life Application Of Brand Marketing: The Crew On The Wall

The Hall was an old empty high school in Philadelphia that hosted after-hour parties on the weekends. You literally go in and smoke, drink, and dance until the sun came up. Inside, the dancehall was the size of a school gymnasium. It was nearly impossible to move inside of the hall. The place was packed to at least three times its capacity. I was a young member of a crew of very important people lets just say. We would control the entire wall of the dance hall, sometimes having over twenty-five people in our entourage. It was the instinct of a criminal to have your back on a wall in places like this to eliminate someone sneaking up from behind and also to avoid being trampled if a gunshot goes off in the party.

Besides the obvious benefits of having our backs to the wall, the wall served us by creating a constant presence in the party. We were on display and became a feature in the club. People wanted to know who we were, while watching young beautiful women gravitate toward our section. The smell of high grade weed also had something to do with people flocking towards us. With up to twenty cigars lit in one section this was bound to happen. Our section became a desired section to be a part of. Customers were gained by our presence in the club. We were selling a lifestyle and weren't even aware of it. People who bought weed from us felt confident about it because of the lifestyle we had achieved because of it. It gave them a sense of hope that they could also achieve the lifestyle they were witnessing.

This would be the result in most of the clubs that we frequented. The lifestyle we lived at night would sometimes be beneficial in the day. The lifestyle was being sold weather we realized it or not. We were enjoying ourselves thoroughly and attracting attention at the same time. It was a great ad for all of our businesses individually. We were profiting off of the feeling we were giving other people. They wanted to be a part of our movement. This is what helped to make the businesses of the guys who leaned on the wall, "Off the wall!"

Lessons from story

Lesson One:
Keep Your Back To The Wall

Keeping your back on the wall means always positioning yourself at a vantage point to see what's happening. It means in all situations be aware of others perception of your business. When fraternizing don't forget that you have to remain mindful of the image being presented. You don't want reality coming up from behind you. It's much better to maintain the ability to control the visuals by controlling your wall. It's about positioning yourself to not look foolish. How would it look for the members in my crew to be uncontrollably trampled if a shot went off? What would people think if they were able to witness someone sneaking up on one of us? These things would have destroyed our image and eventually affected business by appearing vulnerable and weak. Keeping our eyes on the entire situation was a must. It let us know who was with us and who wasn't, which is a safer way of gaining clientele.

Lesson Two:
Our Lifestyle Is For Sale

We were in the club to smoke, drink, and meet women. Who knew that we would gain from doing that. In the business world, your actions, even when you don't know anyone is looking, are for sale. It's a part of the experience you're providing. The atmosphere that you create will resonate with your customer. When selling lifestyles, you should know that your customer wants to feel like they are in the right spot when purchasing. Everything you say and do is a part of the sale. People will closely be watching you to see if the lifestyle that you are selling is comparable to the lifestyle that you're living. Take note of exactly what people are seeing, and you will be able to feed their fantasies. The clothes you wear, the people you associate with, even the weed you smoke, all compiles a lifestyle. Your lifestyle might end up on trial in the eyes of your customer. Always present a good case!

Lesson Three:
Be A Movement

People had become accustomed to us being in the club in our normal position. We became more than a crew of hustlers. We were a movement that people wanted to be a part of. When discussing the club, it would be the girls, the music, and those guys over there. We became a fixture, which grew into a brand. Create a massive presence about yourself and invite others to join in. There's an unspoken criteria that has to be met for being around your business. This might range from hiring people with big personalities to attract customers with big personalities. This is a snowball effect on lifestyle and in business. Remember when dealing with a movement, you either have to move with it or get moved over!

Chapter Six:
Competition:
All is Fair in Hustle & War

What's business without competition? You will most likely have to take a trip to Fantasy Land for the answer. Almost everything associated with business is rooted in competition. That is the angle from which all business is approached. Building an enterprise is a constant state of competition. This doesn't mean that you will be competing with everyone that you encounter, but you will notice the people you meet being split into three separate categories. There will be those that you are in competition with, those that can aid you in your competition, and those that cannot. These categories very simply help you to differentiate what impact you allow for people to have on your business as you engage yourself in these treacherous waters of competition.

In business, competition is warfare, but not every war is fought without diplomacy. Although it should be understood that wars are fought with a great deal of intensity to ensure the survival of one and the demise of another. If you are not prepared for this outcome, then its time for you to hang it up now. Why spend your time building a block that you are not willing to defend? Sometimes war will find its way to you, it's not always something that you have to go out and look for. Sometimes it will knock on your door to see if you deserve your spot. This is the part of business that is not for the weak. It is actually the foundation of business, the flow of competition that pumps through the veins of an enterprise.

People that share your line of work are people that you are engaged in war with. Everyone on the battlefield will not be an enemy. There are some unshakable forces that are solidified, and not engaging in a war for customers with you. Once your status has been solidified, it is better to maintain cordial relations with these types of businesses. Then, there are those that are actively fighting for your customer. This is when you are truly in business. The nature of competition alone can make things more aggressive than normal. Competition starts from the very inception of your product or business idea. From the moment you develop a product you are competing with a previous product. In the case that the product you have is a new invention that has never been seen before, then you are now competing with the void, trying to earn your validation from the marketplace.

The reality is that competition will always exist, knowing this will help you in future competitions that will surely present themselves. Competition can be separated into two categories, offense and defense. These categories are better known in the street by "setting it off" or "being set on". This is the offense and defense of the street and ultimately the world of business. Let's take a look at the two sides of this competitive coin, to gain more perspective on what can be an extremely aggressive setting. Keep in mind that in war even a mouse can make the elephant look silly!

Setting it Off or Getting Set On

Setting it off: Welcome to the home of the alpha. Setting it off on someone is the same as slapping someone. In my opinion, if you're going to slap someone, you better slap the shit out of them! War is not a place for love taps. When you set it off you are telling another business that you are worthy of having their customers. Engaging in competition can be costly, that's why its better to launch damaging blows to your competitors. You should create a presence of fear. When attacking the market, you should be aiming to make everyone look in your direction. You should be exploiting what's different about your business, generating a fear of competing with you. If you launch a big enough or extremely focused attack, you could win the competition in one move. If you create the presence of someone that you don't want to go to war with, people will not see it wise to exhaust resources to fight you. They would rather preserve their funds for the loss of business than lose them defending a clear and calculated attack.

Attacks exist in all aspects of your business. It may even be as simple as having the best design on the street for your store's sign, or the best packaging for your product. Make others wish they had done what you have. You will notice how they shift and begin to move differently post attack. You have to make sure that when you attack, you conquer. In business when you do not fully conquer it can result in your attacks being nothing more than ideas for your opponent. The only way to fully conquer is for the customers and onlookers to know and understand the dominant presence. Remember, when setting it off, if you're going to slap someone, you better slap the shit out of them!

Being set on: When someone sets it off on you this doesn't mean that it is over for you. It means that you have been taken to war by a competitor, and you shouldn't take the situation lightly. Your income stream is being placed into jeopardy, and must now be protected to assure your control over your business. When the stream of income is compromised, someone is benefiting. No one is interested in destroying your business without gaining what they are taking from you. The key to fighting back is remembering that no matter how subtle the attack, it was constructed to disrupt your business. If someone opens a sneaker store on the same street as yours, you best believe they have seen your store and believe they have something better to offer than you do. They may even just be there to benefit from the flow of traffic that you have built. These are all attacks. What about the new jar of peanut butter with the fancy new logo? Wasn't the fancy logo and packaging an attack on the other jars of peanut butter on the shelf? Of course it was, whether you choose to realize it or not!

Sneaky Comp vs Direct

Competition can be very subtle or can also hit you like a ton of bricks. While these are two opposite ways of approaching a situation, the end result is clear. We are engaging in competition. The goal of this competition is to win over customers, and eventually dominate the market. Never forget in business an attack is an attack, whether subtle or flagrant the intention is to win. When we put business in the context of winning and losing it sometimes gives the impression that we are playing a game. It is important that you understand that we are not scoring points and searching for trophies. We are out to win customers, more importantly their money, which fuels our businesses and is the deciding factor of whether we stay afloat while charting our course. If you choose to take the terms winning and losing and apply it to a game, then you should apply it to the games that make up a casino. The stakes are extremely high in this game, if that's what you wish to call it. There are businesses, mortgages, and even children's futures, riding on the line. This is what makes men cry when women can't. Understanding this will help you to understand the nature of an attack, be it subtle or direct. Let's take a separate look at these two different attacks on your enterprise.

Direct Comp: Direct competition is one of the most aggressive aspects of business. It's where there is no mistake, someone is clearly trying to take food off of your plate. Maybe someone is putting a hat store on the same block as yours. The point is the element of opposition is right in your face. When someone places a similar product in the direct vicinity of your product they are telling the customer that their product is good enough to move in, and pretend as if your product never existed. This is an attempt to steamroll. When launching attacks, it is always best to attempt to steamroll your competitor. This applies to every aspect of your business, from creating an ad, to the design of your packaging. You should be trying to knock your competition out. Never try to match the look of what the market currently offers. Raise the bar in your endeavors and your adversaries will get steamrolled in the process. This is how to crush your enemy as a result of boosting your business.

If you find yourself dancing in the ring with someone trying to knock you out of commission with nothing but haymakers, it will be much better to respond with calculated attacks. Throwing wild attacks will exhaust you. Don't rush your response. Make sure you take the time to cook the meal before you serve it. In order to fully understand an attack you have to let it finish exploding first. Trying to respond in the middle of an attack makes it easier for you to end up in the explosion. Let the bomb go off so you can see what is damaged. Not every bomb is as effective as it looks on its way to you. Remember the war is for customers, and they're not all fools. Bottom line, when someone attacks your business boldly, you have to find the point that your opponents weakness meets with your strength so that you can boldly return fire. Never get caught up in games of Tit for Tat.

Sneaky Comp: A wolf in sheep's clothing can do a whole lot of damage. This is the result of sneaky competition. Sneaky competition relies heavily on being emotionally connected with your business. It is so subtle that it will backfire if complained about. Sometimes simply building your business is attacking another. You could take a bucket of paint, freshly paint your storefront and you will see, amongst the compliments there will be those that feel the paint on your building is an attack on their business, creating animosity. You might feel that a bucket of paint is a stretch for creating animosity, but you honestly know that painting your store on a street where others could use it, would create an explosion, and the smell of you shitting on everyone would emanate through the streets.

Don't be a sucker for subtle attacks. Sometimes subtle attacks require bold actions. There are some cases where responding boldly to a subtle attack can appear that you are picking on someone. There are other cases where your bold response will be stomping out your subtle attacker, because subtle attacks are all they were capable of initiating. This will prove highly beneficial to you. The best way to respond to an attack of any kind is with creativity. If someone put out a great commercial, don't try to counter them with a commercial of your own. Take a whole new approach so your attack will be felt without being expected. When your business continues to grow you will find it being often subtlety attacked by a number of adversaries. Sometimes it's best to dominate the situation by finding ways to boldly attack all of your competitors at once.

Cloning

Imitation is the best form of flattery. If that's the case, don't flatter me! Imitating a competitor is a vicious tactic when engaged in a war between businesses. It's not particularly my style, due to preservation of pride. My moral compass won't allow me to abuse such a low down tactic. If you've ever watched two women fight, you know that it's almost a guarantee that one of them is going to pull the hair of the other. There is no mutual understanding in the fight. It may start off with the appearance of mutual combat, but the fight will soon end with all of the rules being bent or broken. The same applies regarding cloning in a business war. It is a dirty tactic that will be applied almost every time at one point or another in the real world of business.

Cloning someone's business model or product is a sure way to end up under the skin of your competitor. When you are engaged in war with a clone, you have to keep a level head before launching attacks and counterattacks. You have to think outside of the box to put your clone where they belong. Because copying the moves you make has become their business model, you have to implement more elusive tactics to win this war. You may have to use words like original, real, or first, to distinguish yourself from a clone. In the street if someone is following your car, you have to find ways to "shake the tail". This is exactly what you must accomplish when dealing with a clone. This is when the creative side of your business should be unleashed. What will your competitor do after the news visits your establishment to speak about work you are doing with a charity in your community? Sounds like a hell of a commercial to me. Do you think the news now wants to visit the shop of someone cloning you and your actions? Your mini-me will be exposed as an imitation.

What about contacting a local celebrity for a photo-op with your product? These are concepts that when beaten to the punch become more difficult than they already are, but are extremely effective in shaking off someone attempting to copy your moves.

If you are attempting to run your business by cloning another, you should be aware that you are possibly creating an early expiration date for your business. When you build your business by copying another, you have to have the money to rub them out completely. There is something about being the original that resonates with people. Large amounts of money can turn you into the bully and have people rally around the underdog. Cloning, copying, and imitating are all extremely evident aspects of business. This is why its best to remain creative and on alert. Remember you can copy the brain, but not the mind. Don't become stale and emotional when engaged in this particular kind of war. You will ultimately end up making emotional decisions that cost more than they're worth.

Emotions

An emotional warrior can be an extremely powerful one. They have the passion required to fully engage in warfare. The key is to be in control of your emotions and not allow your emotions to grow into an adversary of your own. Emotions that run wild can take on a "Frankenstein effect" and become an extra monster to face on the battleground. You have to use your emotions and not be used by them. Being attacked in business can easily trigger an emotional response. Don't allow your emotions to trick you into thinking that you have been attacked personally. A business attack doesn't require a personal response. All a personal response will do for you is get you laughed at, which will most likely lead to more frustration for someone who is not in control of their emotions.

Playing to your strengths is the best way to trigger the emotions of your competitors. This should be the goal when launching attacks. The emotion that we are targeting is fear. When your competition fears you, they make random, sporadic, attacks that only damage their brand by bringing negative attention their way. Fluster your opponents until they make a grand mistake. When you fluster your opponent's emotions you will be able to control them. Your movements will trigger their responses. They are now following you, you might as well lead them into a brick wall. While toying with the emotions of an enemy can become amusing, you can't let this drive your business. Keep your head in the game. Remember, relishing at the stupidity of your opponents emotional outburst, is also an emotion. The joy that you receive after watching a foolish maneuver from an opponent is an emotion that can fluster you as well. You are now entangled in the war and your victory is transforming into a loss for you. There are many ways that our emotions can get the best of us in business. Its better to keep all attacks business related, and use our emotions when executing and not when strategizing. This helps it to become clear when its over and time to move on.

Losing Customers

Losing customers is losing the war. This is why you always need to remember to engage in war with good taste. Don't get caught being to antagonistic with your competition. You will draw negative attention towards your business. Its better to force a clear victory than to pick on someone daily. Picking on the competition sheds light on them and in doing so makes customers wonder why they are a worthy adversary. When businesses are at war they are at war for customers. Someone is going to gain customers and someone will lose customers. Constantly going back and fourth with a competitor will eventually pique the curiosity of the customer. This will give the opposing business the opportunity to make a lasting impression on them that is often motivated by the attack from their competitor. This increases their chance of destroying your credibility in the process, thus the loss of a customer. You must make valid attempts to convince your customers that you are better than your competitor and move on. Don't allow your customers to trap you into performing in daily battles that don't benefit your business.

If you are losing significant amounts of customers then you are losing the war. You might have to alter your business in ways that go completely against your initial business plan. It might mean switching your intended demographic. It might be better in the midst of a losing war to push your business into a more exclusive direction to gain a new customer base. If you're already in an exclusive environment, the opposite may suit you better. The point to understand is that war can change your circumstances dramatically. You have to be willing to change things to allow profits to resume, while managing to keep your head on straight. Just because a customer leaves, doesn't mean they won't be back. You have to be able to keep your business running in the midst of the chaos. The easiest way to lose a war is to stop fighting. Once your loss of customers provokes you into a slump where you begin opening late and leaving early, you have been defeated. Your business is similar to the lottery in the effect that you can't win if you don't play. If you give up and leave early, that chance of the big spender coming through your door has been eliminated. You've just thrown away your ticket before looking to see if you've won or not.

Real Life Application Of Setting It Off & Being Set On

One thing that I have been since my mid teens was connected. I could always get my hands on product. I would always make it clear that I was the most trust worthy outlet that a connect could find. This gave me access to being given a higher ranking than my financial status warranted because my honor, principle, and ethic held value in the streets amongst those who looked for these characteristics. It would more than likely be someone with a higher status in the game to recognize these traits. Lower level workers were consumed by the nature of being cowboy, and pirate like. Those traits might help you earn a fierce reputation, but can't help you along the lines of progression.

The connections that I had, made things a whole lot easier for me to steamroll competition. If you were a legit business I would keep a respectful distance, meaning one block, or around the corner. I wasn't going to setup next door to you. The fact is you were going to lose business regardless. When we set it off, we're taking over, plain and simple. The product, the consistency, and the discipline was enough to run competition out of business, or almost out of business. My attitude towards them was always that they don't exist. We were competing with ourselves. They were competing with us. Our packaging and our product was not tailored to the other people selling product. It was us employing the strategies available to us, which were limitless.

When my partner told me he wanted to use jars instead of bags for mid grade weed I thought he was crazy. High grade weed would come in a glass jar and mid to low grade came in a bag. That's the way that things were done in the streets all over the east coast. He found a spot that had plastic jars with a cylinder shape that could be filled to the top. It actually had less space then a dime bag and gave our premium product a premium look. Even on days when we were forced to sell a bullshit product the brand survived. This particular run was a phenomenal one indeed. We flooded the streets with plastic jars that came from one corner, and one corner only. Tens of thousands of dollars were made over the course of a summer.

One day in the height of our operation it was obvious that business had slowed down. We had felt it for about a week but on this particular afternoon we said we barely made money this morning "What the fuck?!" In the middle of making a whole lot of money and having a third of South Philly buying weed from us, we got a little bit too comfortable. We took to the streets to get to the bottom of the problem and found out we were being cloned for about a week. Someone did their homework and had a connect. We had something that he didn't have, and was infringing upon, and that was real estate. We rented a building and payed for our real estate, which meant that he had to go. He didn't have a team, and didn't have anywhere to be close enough to us, but would cut off traffic with the same product while on a bike. He was putting me back to work to defend the castle. I knew if my customers saw my face they were coming to me, plain and simple. After all, we built the neighborhood. Well, that was true for some and not for all. Some customers want the name they trust, some want to walk half a block less for the same thing.

It was now time to exercise the right to push someone with no real estate out of the vicinity. While his roaming around could be dangerous as well. He was a parasite picking away at what we had taken the time to cook. We stepped to him and told him he had to move and that he couldn't pull a customer off of our block. His only option was to go build another block somewhere else, not approach someone else's customers like a scavenger. He agreed to move on but was caught the very next day making sales. My partner came in the spot early one afternoon and told me to come with him to have a talk with this guy. We finally linked up, and it was now a group of angry young men fighting over real estate, armed with more than hot tempers. It wasn't long before the wrong words flew and the shots followed. That day a car, a stop sign, and a brick wall were all injured in this altercation, luckily for us all. With no real estate to retreat to and knowing that they were now a wide open target, our competition packed up and left.

The truth of the matter is that he didn't have to. He could have forced another result. While it wasn't fair of him to take customers from us after we hugged the block to build it, it was fair for him to do it at the same time. Fair is determined by your moral compass and we don't always share the same values. You may end up at war with an animal that wants to take your business and make you starve. It doesn't matter if you own an ice cream parlor or a candy store, you might have to "buss a shot" today. No, I don't mean literally from a gun, but you may have to defend what you have built. You might be inventing a sale that your competition can't afford to regain your customer, but you sometimes have to fire a shot to wake everybody up. This is business. For those of you who consider yourselves to be non confrontational my brother always told me, if your scared of confrontation don't come outside.

Lessons from story

Lesson One:
War Happens When It Happens

Someone who is launching an attack on your business is not waiting for it to be the perfect time for you, it's the perfect time for them. This is why when businesses are attacked it often leaves the feeling of "Why is this happening now?" It's because that's the perfect time for your adversary, that's why. The attack that was launched on me could have never happened during the building stages of this block. In this stage I was extremely focused and would have constantly been manning my operation. While building, we left no stones unturned and had no weaknesses exposed. Our very own success became a weakness. It provided luxuries that were not there when we were building our business. These weaknesses are opportunities for those in competition with you. You have to learn to let your money work for you and not weaken you. You should be using money to setup a structure that only money could setup before attempting to enjoy it. Build a castle!

You don't have the option to tell people you're too tired for war. When they set it on you, your in it! Whether you win or lose, you'll be able to carve out a spot of your own. Depending on your nature, this fact might work in your favor. You may want to take a business out so you can make money. You may see a weakness and launch an attack of your own. As long as you aren't crossing any moral boundaries, good luck to you. As long as you keep it all business, it's all business. If you're setting it off on someone, you can't let them tell you when to do it. If that were the case, your secretary will be scheduling meetings for attacks on your business, which is highly unlikely.

Lesson Two:
Customers And Connects Aren't Involved

When you're at war, YOU'RE at war! You may have allies such as a loyal customer or a connect that wants to see you win, but the war is yours to fight. Your customer is not concerned with your light bill, or what you have gone thru the trouble of building. They are concerned with getting the best that they can get for the lowest they can get it for, and will go with most convenient method of achieving that goal. When you are in a fight to keep a customer, you can't expect the customer to help. When customers become aware of competition it becomes leverage for them. They are only on your team if your the only game in town. Loyal customers do exist, but you can't expect them not to try to benefit from a war. That would go against the nature of a customer. You have to find creative ways to keep their attention. When they get wind of who is authentic, the choice will become more clear for them and business will resume. This is a key reason you should be saving money. Wars can be expensive!

Your connect wants you to succeed for obvious reasons, but a war can shift things around in ways that make it hard for them to help you. Don't assume you're going to be able to bring your connect down in the trenches with you. They maintain a different status than you, and your relationship is predicated on you selling their product. They may extend different ways to offer some aid, but it's not their responsibility to keep you afloat. The best way to stop these attacks is to remain vigilant of what's going on surrounding your business. Don't give the opportunity for negative situations to grow into a bigger problem.

Lesson Three:
It's All Fair

All is fair in love and business. You can yell out "that's not fair" all you want. The fact is, its happening. Being fair doesn't exist in the middle of a war. Don't make the mistake of thinking that everyone shares your moral perspective. Stealing ideas and concepts may seem like a perfectly good idea to someone else, and taking your customers might seem like an even better one. You have to be prepared for all of these instances by being prepared for one thing, and that is to fight. You've got to be ready to get down and dirty. It doesn't matter how expensive your outfit is, if you want to buy another, you may have to get the one you're wearing dirty in defense of what's yours. Building what you are not willing to defend is building something for someone else. War is nothing short of competition at the highest level. Once involved in a war, spoils are a plus, your real reward is survival. Make sure you don't get caught in the middle of the battlefield worried about what is and what isn't fair. Secure you victory first and discuss the ethical practices of your adversaries later. Remember, when its on its on!

Summary: The Bucwild Words of Star

One of the most valuable lessons that I've learned in business regarding competition was gained from a meeting with radio personality and owner of the "Star & Bucwild Morning Show", Star. I had taken a meeting with him to discuss his possible role in a film project that I was looking to get off the ground. Being a hustler, I knew that you had to have a product and I worked vigorously on creating a script that I felt was strong enough to be put into production. For years I had envisioned myself escaping the drug trade and being able to secure a place for myself in the legitimate world of business. While the drive to finally obtain a legal business of my own filled my being, I began chipping away on a movie script in between drug sales. All the years I've spent in the street helped me to understand the power of a product, and I knew if this script was to get me where I wanted to be, it had to be right.

After completing what I deemed a masterpiece, I fired off an email to the famous morning show host requesting a meeting to propose the project. Star wasn't hard to get in contact with if you were looking to talk business. He kept his ears to the streets making him a prime target for hungry entrepreneurs. What separated him from other celebrity hosts was his accessibility. He accepted my request and granted me a meeting later in the week. I printed out the script in its entirety and prepared for the meeting.

Walking into this meeting I had no idea what to expect. I was there fueled by the hunger of leaving the streets. Being seasoned in the streets himself, Star could see us coming from a mile away. My intention was to allow him to read the script in his own time and then respond if interested. There were a few other scenarios involved that I won't get into in this particular story. Understanding product gave me the confidence of knowing that he would be interested if he read the work in its entirety. Of course this was not the case. He opted not to read a single word of the script for legal reasons that I understood completely when explained. He did offer some advice regarding moving forward. It was when I asked him for some information on how to shop my product without having it stolen in the process that he gave me a jewel that I held onto to this very day. His answer was short and straight to the point, "...I mean respectfully, people stole from Michael Jackson, who the fuck are you?" The ego that the streets created ran wild in my head. I thought, he has no idea what I will do if someone steals what I've built, he's gotta be crazy.

It was days later that his words began to set in completely. In business, stealing is a part of the game. It may be an ugly part that is frowned upon by most, but it still exists. There has to be more where that came from. If you make movies and someone steals your movie, whether you seek vengeance or not, the show must go on.

You have to be prepared for people to take your style, clone your actions, and try to appear the same way that you do if you want to be great. That is something that is attached to greatness. It was these words that helped me in later endeavors to acknowledge the theft of my style from a new angle. My first thought was always "Of course you want to steal my style, I'm the shit!"

Chapter Seven:
Sucker Free: Soaring with Turkeys

When dealing with me, you have now entered a "Sucker Free" zone. My training in the street has given me a navy seal status in business. My ability to spot a sucker has been heightened due to my vigorous training in the boot camps of the block. Remaining "sucker free" is a huge component to gaining success. It requires a keen eye towards the personality traits of others. In the street, there are many negative situations that are summed up by simply calling it "Sucka Shit". We have all been a victim of a sucker or experienced some sucker shit. I've compiled a list of their personality traits to explore in this chapter. This may quite possibly prove to be some of the most impactful information in business you will find, because nothing can destroy a business like the behavior of a sucker can!

Liars

The liar breaks a fundamental law of business. When dealing with a liar it is extremely hard to conduct business while outside of their presence. Doing business with them means that when you leave their company, or hang up the phone with them, the trust level will not be strong enough to operate free of discomfort. The lie is a sign of disrespect because it creates an uneven playing field to work on. It can be as simple as saying you're going to be somewhere at a certain time, while knowing you will be late. It might also be as extreme as lying about a payment. Business relies on the truth being told to control waste. The size of the lie can significantly contribute to the damage accumulated, but all lies in the business world contribute to waste. It can range from wasted time, wasted money, to even wasting gas. In business, waste must be controlled. Imagine you have a sink that is constantly dripping. You must stop the leak to stop the waste. The liar is very similar to the dripping sink. The waste created must be stopped at the source.

The business world is intertwined with the world of liars because of the many self serving motives invoked by it. People are concerned with the success of their own business, first and foremost. Telling lies to suppliers and customers can be a normal practice for some people, regardless of the lack of ethics that it entails. Someone who tells small lies will eventually tell bigger ones, that may eventually affect your business negatively. What you have to remember is while it may exist in the business world, it's not business protocol, so it is up to you to be the rule of law for what you will and will not accept to properly control waste that will negatively affect your business.

Mommas Boys

Now we may be entering the realm of psychology, but we are not leaving the realm of business. The "momma's boy" is the business person who is not ready for the business world. The world of business is the real world magnified. Momma's boys are those who haven't experience the real world without a safety net, so the rough waters of business is enough to drown them instantly. Training one, can be far more difficult than training an independent person. These people are use to a level of comfort that has been provided for them. In business, comfort is earned and fought for. Training them requires undoing all of the pampering that was done to them and can be an exhausting task for the owner. When speaking to these types of people you will find they are extremely intimidated by a stern tone of voice because it greatly differs from the tone of a caring mother. They also believe heavily in second and third chances because that is what has been given to them in their extended home life. You may find yourself attempting to work around this personality trait by softening your speech or giving multiple chances to finish simple tasks. At this point you are only prolonging their departure from your business. It is unhealthy for adults to live in a child state under the guidance of their parents, and it is just as unhealthy for a business owner to try to facilitate this kind of behavior.

When taking a closer look into the lives of people who are taken care of, the fact that they are horrible employees will avail itself to you undoubtedly. The Momma's boy lives in a world where Mom takes care of everything. Can you imagine dealing with someone who thinks this way when it comes to business? Well, if you haven't already, you most likely will. It's just that you haven't been able to put your finger on why you are being guided towards speaking softer and more gently to someone who is not efficient and slowing down your production. It's not your job to do this. Let Mom handle it!

In Love

It's great to be in love. There's nothing wrong with it. In fact, its actually quite healthy. What people that are in love fail to realize is that their significant other is of great importance to them, and is not as important to those who are not in love with them. This can very easily become an extremely convoluted situation. It's the "silent partner that speaks loudly" scenario, with a partner you had no idea that you were partners with. The spouse of your partner or person you are in business with is often injected into your affairs unfairly. This changes the initial agreement because someone involved has changed from who they were at the initial stages of your business' growth. Understanding this principle can be a life or death matter when speaking in terms of your business. Know that your spouse is special to you, and focus on what special means. Everyone can't take part in special, that would go against its meaning.

Business involves people, plain and simple, and people have loved ones. It's your job to remember that you are not in business with their loved ones. There is nothing wrong with taking occasional advice from a partner's spouse, but you should ask yourself this before proceeding. How many times does someone want to hear, "My wife thinks that..." or "my husband said we should..."? People are often polite in these situations because of the very delicate nature of them, but these things can snowball if gone unaddressed. When confronted with this, you should know that it is not a personal attack if someone is telling you things related to your spouse, because you are the one who added them into the lives of your partners. Your spouse is your partner, not your partners' partner. This should be clear, so that it is understood that using these people for excuses won't suffice.

"Sorry I'm late for the meeting, my wife was taking too long to get ready." "Sorry I missed that phone call, I was out with my husband on the beach." These may sound like perfectly good excuses to you, but to your partners it is nothing but bullshit. People who are in love don't understand the signals they send. What they are saying is that there is now someone who has captivated too much of their attention for the business to grow. It has so much of their attention that they feel it should have your attention as well. When frequently attaching a spouse to your excuses, you are implying that they are more important than the needs of your business. Of course our loved ones' lives are more important than our business, but only on a large scale. Things that are not life threatening to your spouse should not interfere with what might be life threatening to your business. Love your spouse after work, and love them during work by working diligently at your job to provide comfort in both of your lives. Remember, being in love with your business is being in love with success!

Smart Money

Smart money is when the presidents on the bills in your pockets have a lower I.Q than the presidents on the bills of those around you. This renders their money smarter than yours. Your money will be able to take all of the risks, while their money makes more calculated and sophisticated decisions. This mentality can strain a partnership because it unequally distributes stress to the owners. There are some people who will allow you to buy them a coffee everyday without offering to buy one for you. With the exception of someone who has been vocal about their negative financial state, this is a case of smart money.

The owners of smart money will watch others spend like a spectator in the bleachers. They tend to be very calm and reserved when money is talked about. You might be asking yourself, what's wrong with this? It's better to be smart with money, right? The answer is yes, you should be smart with your money. The problem lies when you are not being smart with the money of your partners. If you have reservations or hear things that make you skeptical of spending your money, you should be vocal about it so that your partner understands clearly why you are not willing to invest. Allowing your partner to do this without speaking up is abuse. You are using them to gamble for you. If there is a loss, it's not yours, and if there is a gain, you will profit from it. Give your partners the opportunity to convince you to spend the money, and take the time to convince them not to.

When in business with someone, you have gone to war with them. The goal is for everyone to make it home. You have to share information with the soldiers in your army to be able to effectively strategize together. Withholding effort can also be as dangerous as withholding information or money. If you have not fully expressed your doubts verbally you are inevitably going to pull back on your efforts. Make sure you allow your partner the chance to fully explain their vision to you to gain trust in this particular project. Don't treat your money as if it is smarter than the money of those you are in business with, and beware of this around you. We all would like to have short arms and deep pockets at some point or another, but you can't allow your partners to gamble alone.

Crumb Snatchers

The crumb snatcher is synonymous with the bottom feeder. The problem with bottom feeders is that out of all of the vastness the ocean has to offer, the bottom feeder has brought you into the dark, and murky waters of the bottom. This is where the shit falls. You have now entered the world of the unlucky and unfortunate. The unfortunate things that happen to them will now be inadvertently happening to you. The bottom feeder's world is an accountability free zone. The conditions at the bottom are obvious enough to see that your business is not insured. This is especially true when dealing with consignment.

Giving a bottom feeder a consignment is nothing short of a gamble. They are unable to pay for their own mishaps. They don't own things and have no way of covering the possessions of others. Their desperate conditions must not be ignored because it impairs their judgment in business settings. They are people that out of necessity listen to their stomachs over the voices of reason and logic. You must be careful when working with people that are too close to the edge. You need partners and clients who are capable of making sound decisions that create more prosperous situations.

This crumb snatching mentality relies heavily on sympathy of their circumstances. This is dangerous to be around because it won't allow them to be sympathetic of situations that are stressful to you. They are too close to the bottom to feel sympathy for the fish that swim above them. Even when you are put into a precarious position in your business, the bottom feeder will be right there waiting for the next handout. They have no other way to eat, making them dependent on what falls to the bottom.

Being at the bottom is different from being a bottom feeder. These are people who are comfortable and thrive at the bottom. When doing so, it is not a concern of theirs where the food is coming from. They rarely are loyal to one connect and will work with anyone willing to come to the bottom to feed them. Sometimes they are needed in business to help get rid of low quality products that will not satisfy the rest of the ocean. It's when you get too comfortable around them that their misfortunes will become yours, and they won't hesitate to welcome you to the bottom. Don't think that they will keep you company there either. They will be off looking for someone else to come close to the bottom before dinner!

Flashy

The best way for me to describe flashy people in business is to explain the power of a uniform. A uniform commands attention and respect. It means that you are a part of an exclusive environment. It doesn't matter if it is the uniform of a decorated marine war hero or the uniform of a Mc Donald's manager, it commands respect in its proper environment. The uniform can also create a false presence of ability. Every football player on the team does not possess the same ability, yet they all are wearing the very same uniform. When we look past the uniform into the actions of the player, we can then adequately determine the difference of ability. Ironically in football it is not a good thing to have a shiny new uniform with no marks on your helmet. It means that you were sitting on the bench the entire time.

Every business has a uniform and we can't allow them to play tricks on our eyes. It doesn't matter if you're a street hustler, or a doctor, we're all out here in uniforms. Should you judge your connect by the type of car they drive? Does having a great suit mean that you are a great surgeon? The answers are obvious, yet when faced with these scenarios the mind reacts to visuals. We are sometimes blinded by the uniform of someone in our own field. Just because someone has all the latest equipment or dresses the part doesn't mean they are willing to put in the work. For instance, every fireman is not going to rescue the cat from the tree. Some of them are going to say, "Look lady, don't worry. He'll come down" and keep going.

What people must understand about the flashy business person is that it doesn't necessarily equal skill. In the case that skill is not providing their expensive lifestyles, something else is. Don't let it be you! Flashy in business means one of two things. Either you are making beyond the average amount of money, or you want people to think you are. This can become a lie without words that they are allowing others to believe. People see nice cars and clothes and become more inclined to do business with someone because it provides a feeling of insurance on your product. Often times, these flashy individual's are very similar to the bottom feeder. The difference is all of their money as well as some of yours is going towards feeding their desires. Take a good look at their flashy possessions because you might end up making the payments on some of them.

Most importantly, don't allow these types of people to distract you. Make sure you maintain control of your mind when around such extravagant things. These people are all about perception and won't tell you the negative side they may be experiencing. You will end up competing with someone who doesn't have food in the refrigerator, or someone who is swamped in debt. Its normal to be impressed by success. It is an issue of making sure that it is success that's impressing you, and that you haven't allowed yourself to be merely blinded by the flash!

Party Goers

Put your dancing shoes on! When you do business with those who can't control their party appetite, you should party with them. This way you will at least be able to smile while your business suffers. Business requires boundaries. Each person involved must have a set of guidelines that they follow. Of course you may have earned the right to go out and blow off some steam. This is not to be confused with the actions of a Party Goer. They party by way of ritual. It might be every weekend or every day, but it is something that is engrained in them, a must do. Imagine someone who goes to a bar everyday after work. Before they have left work for the day their mind is already on a barstool. The constant party goer is not in the right mind frame for business. Business requires focus and dedication that cannot run parallel to continuos clubbing.

How would you like to pay for some parties that you won't be attending? Unfortunately this is the cost of doing business with these types of people. They are those that party for a living and do business on the side. Business is not their first priority. Their days begin exhausted from the previous evening and mentally unfocused and often end thinking of what's to come after leaving work. The result is someone who is going to leave a strain on others for the sake of a party. While you may not be in charge of someone's personal life, how it effects your business, is your business. Even constantly discussing this type of lifestyle in the workplace can be a distraction to others. It's completely counter productive to the agenda of a business.

Responsible business people set timelines of focus and simply don't party within those parameters. Don't misconstrue this with having a drink or smoking weed. I'm speaking about clubs, cocktail parties, concerts, etc. by way of ritual. This generates slack, and that slack must be taken up by someone. That someone can only be someone responsible enough to do so. You should always try to surround yourself with those that share the same focus that you do. You will be able to get much further with people that are more concerned with owning clubs than attending them.

Lazy Asses

You must be on the lookout for part time employees that are on the clock full time. Before the politically correct times that we live in now, corporations had exercise facilities to help their employees stay in shape. It was more than just keeping down the cost of insurance. It's because being overweight represented a lazy attitude that didn't comply with what the business asked of them. This doesn't mean that everyone that is overweight is lazy. I'm speaking about the perception given by them aiding the corporations' decision to have employees exercise. The fact is, the thinnest person in your company may very well be the laziest.

Laziness among other things can corrode your business from within. Lazy people require rewards and incentives to do basic tasks. They will do the minimum required, and in some cases fall short of it. Work is not a priority for them, so working for someone else will not bring out the best in them. Laziness creates disdain inside of work environments. Customers, coworkers, employees, and partners can all be a victim of the same lazy business person. It is a very dangerous condition because it doesn't require them to be preoccupied with anything. They simply create the luxury of not caring. They don't care what the customer thinks, nor are they concerned with meeting the business' needs. In some cases they allow for dirt to pile up and still believe that there is nothing to do. They are constantly in search of moments when there is nothing for them to do. In business there is always something to do! This doesn't mean expecting employees to care for your business in the same way that you do, but you have to be careful not to fall victim to these traits. Being lazy is very different from not being as committed as others. It is up to you to decide what you will consider to be laziness in your own environment. One thing a lazy person will not call themselves in these instances is lazy. It calls for termination, so the lazy individual will attempt to disguise their laziness with excuses. How many excuses will depend on how many you choose to allow.

Scary People

What scares you doesn't have to scare me. In fact, what scares you might make me laugh. As a business owner you have to remove fear from your equation. People who deal with fear at times can project their fears onto someone else that they are doing business with. They will tell you what you are doing can't be done. They are not comfortable confronting their own fears and feel that others should be just as cautious as they are. Nervous movements and constant hesitation can stifle the progress of your business. You can't achieve success without the element of risk. I'm not at all saying you shouldn't be prepared, but spending too much time preparing for what you cannot prepare for is not a good practice. You might have to beat your chest and dive in.

While a cautious voice can sometimes be the voice of reason, you don't need someone in the room talking you out of every move you make. Business requires confidence. Your customers and colleagues can tell when you are uncertain about something. It's a warning sign for them, telling them they should be just as nervous as you are. Make sure to make clear decisions so that others can feed off of your confidence. Mistakes will be made, fearing them will not lead to progress. You have to have a thicker layer of skin in the business world. Be ready to succeed and accept that failure is a part of the process. Learning from your failures will help you to become a seasoned entrepreneur.

Be aware that fear is contagious because it is natural. It's not a foreign feeling, so we are sometimes tricked into thinking we are right to be fearful. Fear is used to protect us from harm. Being fearful of outcomes in business can change the energy needed to succeed. Picture a team in a locker room before a championship game. What good is fear going to do in this situation? Picture a team member spreading fear and doubt amongst his teammates before they leave the locker room. This person has now clouded the minds of the team and lessened their chances of winning. That is very different from being wise and sensible. Instead they have let their fears cripple their teammates before the game. Treat your office like a locker room by making sure your team is all on the same chord before leaving the room. You should be pumped up and ready to win like a champion. Remember, in the Land of Biz the cowardly lion is not who you want to walk down the yellow brick road to success with you!

Jump Shippers

In business you have to work hard on building a team. Even when you think you're running a one man operation, you're not. There will always be other people that interact with your enterprise, and this is your team. You have to be sure that your team is not scoring points for the other team, meaning that everybody is focused on winning. Spotting someone scoring points for the other team is not as easy as spotting someone who is willing to change teams. These are known as jump shippers. When the ocean current gets too rough they will jump onto another ship that is sailing more comfortably and leave their crew behind.

Getting nervous while encountering troubled times is natural, jumping ship isn't. If you can't weather the storm with your team you shouldn't be able to share in their success. No one wants to be on the losing team, but the answer is not jumping ship. Its better to work with your team to become winners and create a team that is desired to be a part of. Business can be very aggressive and cut throat. Having a team around you makes it easier to navigate through these situations. With everyone on the same page, it creates a presence of dominants. It lets others know that there is no weak link in your chain to pull on, making success easier to achieve.

Pay attention to people in your business that hold other businesses in high esteem. Learning from other businesses is a good thing to do, but wishing you were on their team is not fair to your teammates. If you want success go out and get it. Don't hang around others waiting to see if they get there, jumping from team to team. You will be branding yourself as a jump shipper, and nobody wants one for a teammate. Once someone has jumped ship they should never be allowed to return under the same conditions. They must work diligently at a lower position to earn back the trust of those they've abandoned.

Fuck Ups

A fuck up is someone who exhibits multiple traits of the sucker, without specializing in any one. For example, they don't lie enough to be called a liar, and they're not lazy enough to be described as lazy. They might not be flashy all the time, but they will be flashy at the wrong time. This is a fuck up. They are people that are hard to get angry with because the mistakes they make are not intentional. The biggest mistake is on your behalf, having them around your business. They don't provide the comfort of knowing things are being done correctly. They often attempt to cover up the mistakes they've made or trivialize them. They rarely understand the magnitude of what they are messing up and think that everything can be fixed.

Putting your business in the hands of a fuck up is the easiest way to become one. Simply stated, letting them take the wheel is fucking up. Do yourself a favor and rid them from your business. You may have friends or family that fit this description. Keep them away from your business. Don't give them the chance to destroy what you are building. Let them share stories with you of times that they have fucked things up outside of your business. It's ok to laugh at the stories but do your best not to become one.

Real Life Application of Sucker Free: Get Out!!!

At the age of nineteen, I found myself on a financial roller coaster. There were great moments and there were also some moments that helped to create the monster that I am today. In the winter of 99' my pockets went empty. I was living in North Philly with my brother and some friends. One day I couldn't take the hunger pains and decided to go into South Philly where my partner and I had previously had a few monumental runs. I remember walking through the streets in the rain until spotting a for rent sign in a window of a first floor apartment, just feet away from a corner I used to work. I had a gut feeling that I may have been pressing my luck, but chose to let my stomach guide me and do my best to control the situation. I got the number and constructed the plan in my head. This was not my first time to this dance. I knew everything it would take to get this off the ground. All that was left was to approach the investors and suppliers.

I went to the spot where the investors and suppliers were hanging out to present the idea. Having no money, I would have to sell them on the fact that I was capable of running this operation, just merely needed the rental fee and the product. I managed to convince them, but couldn't convince my previous partner to join us. This time I was again alone, but I was focused. The money was given to me to secure the place, and that I did. I did my best trying to convey that I could man this operation. Since I didn't have money I had to sell my value. I was looking for an ownership stake in exchange for scouting the building, recruiting the workers, and being willing to build the spot. My request for ownership was answered with a vague promise, but I was broke and willing to work to turn that into the yes that I desperately needed.

My connect came with me to the rental office to rent the spot. I'm guessing I wasn't as convincing as I thought I was. Coming into the office with a thick Trinidadian accent wasn't the smartest decision, that he quickly realized when the landlord kept repeating "No drugs". In our world it was "just give us the keys". He hesitantly gave us the keys and the lease, and after doing so, it immediately became go time. I don't know why my connects felt the need to do so, but they had decided to come and hug the block with me. Part of them wasn't fully confident in my ability, and the other side of them wanted to prove to themselves that they still had it in them. This lasted about two hours, and three police cars driving by before they decided to pack up and let me run the show.

The spot was now mine, and the value I was trying to prove ended up being proven by them. I was in and out of the building using a combination of hugging the block and hugging the spot, and without a doubt business was growing. My connects would sometimes come to hang out and observe my progress. After seeing it build up they decided to implement a few professional touches. They came in and scoured the spot to put in a stash spot for the money and the product. It was now officially up and running, and this is when the problems came in. It brought out the usual suspects. These were certain friends that were more friends then business partners. I was just coming out of financial ruin and was in charge of managing the spot, not to mention my name was on the lease and on the line as well.

I was not interested in hiring friends. I was looking to work with a serious crew of workers to build the spot into an official place of business. Instead I was sent workers from my connect who turned out to be all friends, but also bad employees also. They individually or collectively could never be able to do what I had done by convincing the connects to open this spot, yet they were all there. I chose to bring in a worker of my own who I knew from a previous corner was capable of handling the workload. I was chastised for it, and was told I should be looking out for members of my crew. All I could think was this was not the time to enlist the "Bad News Bears", I could go to jail. I didn't argue as much as I should have and ended up coaching the team.

If it wasn't the radio being too loud or too many people in the spot, it was too much back and fourth to the store, in and out of the door. This kind of shit made my skin crawl. Running a spot is just as much aggressive as it is delicate. The people I was managing would always show up after the spot had been built. They had no idea what was truly required to build an organization. This is who I was forced to work with. One of my friends in particular was not sent by the connect. He was not even on the payroll. He would use friendship as a way of lingering around the business. When it came to hustling he had no resume. He had untrustworthy ways and made any responsible manager have to keep their eyes on him. He was an internal distraction that was in the way of progress.

One evening I planned to sneak away after midnight to spend the night with a girl I was dating at the time. The streets were quiet and my band of misfits were all preparing to leave for the night. It was just after midnight when we were leaving out of the door and I was approached by my friend that was of no use. He wanted to stay there with a girl that he was seeing. To add more fuel to the fire. I had just gotten a pound of weed that needed to be bagged up earlier that day and had it in the stash. Instead of telling him "No" and being done with it, I told him he could stay, but I took the pound out of the stash because I knew he was going to go in there as soon as we left, looking for weed to smoke. I dropped the weed in the trunk, planning to bag it at the girls apartment, and we all piled into the car. We made it about three blocks away before the car was pulled over. We all sat on the curb while the car was searched and the weed was discovered. I was faced with the dilemma that I knew my friend wouldn't understand. To this day I'm not sure if I made the right or wrong decision, but he was arrested with the pound of weed because it was in his car.

Before you close this book and throw it away, let me explain my logic for not jumping up to claim the weed and take the charge. I honestly felt that it wasn't fair or smart for me to work to build up the spot, hire incompetent friends that had no idea that they were in the way, and then jump up and take the charge for weed that they too were going to make money off of. Not to mention the fact that they were the reason why the police were watching so closely. If I went to jail that night the spot would have instantly crumbled. I knew he should be out in no more than two days and made a decision that I still wrestle with to this day.

The South Philly narcotics division just had their suspicions confirmed. I was pissed off because I knew that it was the actions of the people around me that caused the place to heat up with police attention. They thought they understood hustling and were really unable to fully put their heads in the game because they had no idea what they were doing. Too many leather jackets and not enough blending in to get the job done. On top of it all, I was the one who had to make the call to the connect and tell them that the product they just dropped off was gone. I ended up with a gun in my face that night. It wasn't a big deal because I knew they were angry, but not crazy. I smoothed that situation out and agreed to get back to work, minus my partner status that I had been diligently working to achieve.

That morning I could feel the heat. I was so in tune with the block I could feel the police without seeing them. Another friend of mine who was sent from the connect had a bundle that he asked me to let him sell from the spot. This was a no no. It was all wrong because it wasn't fair to the people paying the rent for the spot, and it also confused the customer who came for a specific quality, but they sent him. I told him to sit with me for a few days and watch closely to learn the customers, and only sell to people he had seen me sell to because he had poor judgement. In an effort to stop my friends from going in and out of the door, that day I took a store order and walked to the store. I returned from the store and took my seat closest to the door. I knew that I was the only one who would jump up for the sales. My friends thought I was being greedy but I was actually trying to get the customer off of the steps as quickly as possible.

I would answer every knock like clockwork until one specific knock came. The funny thing is it was no different from the rest. I told them to let it go and ignore it. My friend said he would get it because he could unload his crap on them. Letting him insist, I got up and said, "Who is it?" an older man replied "It's Papi." I'm now saying aloud "Who the fuck is Papi?" My friend says, "Oh, Papi I just sold him two." He opens the door and six of Philadelphia's finest come rushing into the spot. Apparently my friend didn't know that when I told him I was going to the store, that wasn't code for sell an undercover officer two bags of weed from the house.

The police searched the apartment for almost an hour before finding the stash. We headed off to jail and I felt like the fool that I had become. My connect bailed us out the next day and I returned to the block. I chose to hustle outside calmly for several reasons. First off, there was the fact that I was now broke again, and there were customers that were still there. I knew I couldn't open the spot again for business. I went back to the method I had employed in the past and took to the corner. This made it easier to see the police coming. My friend who had helped to cause all of this madness wanted to join me. I wanted to tell him to go as far away from me as possible but didn't. I allowed him to post up on the corner with me. We ended up in jail later that day, but not as a result of anything that we had done wrong. We were snitched on by a woman whose window faced my outside stash spot. This woman would under normal circumstances be a lookout for me, but since her daughter was recently arrested she used me for a bargaining chip.

My friend couldn't take the blame for this one, but I knew his presence was a serious problem. I couldn't function at my highest capacity with inefficient people around who were there because of friendship and sympathy. By the way, none of them had ever been successful at hustling from that point on. After coming out of jail for the second time in three days I was full of anger. I saw my connects and unleashed on them my true feelings. I told them I would never work with those kinds of people again, and friendship was not business, if they wanted to work with them feel free. My connect listened and laughed. He knew that jail hadn't scared me away from hustling, it scared me away from incompetent people. He looked at me and knew I was much closer to being him than I was to being them.

Lessons from story

Lesson One:
Trust Your Gut

The truth is that I could actually feel the business. I knew that having three or four people leaving at once was not smart. I knew that loud music playing in the spot was wrong. You have to be able to hear the street to take the pulse. I knew that I shouldn't have tried to transport drugs at night. The point I am making is that there were a lot of things that I knew, but was doing the opposite. I had all of these gut feelings that I was ignoring because of friendship. I understood that if I would have run the place the right way the police would have moved on to a new target. The time that I spent watching over the actions of other people should have been spent listening to my own gut. The feelings there were real. I was the only one focused on the spot. Since the minds of my associates were preoccupied with delusions of grandeur, why shouldn't I have listened to my gut?

When you choose to listen to outside sources and go against your gut, make sure they are credible. After all, make sure you're not ignoring your feelings to spare the feelings of those who are not focused on your business. Your gut has your best interest at heart, make sure that you have a damn good reason not to listen to it if you choose not to. "I told you so" can be a very expensive statement. Listening to your gut is much more cost effective. Its like having your own personal lawyer, insurance agent, doctor, and best friend, listening in on the huddle. In essence, it is the strongest player on your team. Don't make it sit on the bench!

Lesson Two:
Put Your Foot Down

Every time that I wanted to yell out "Get the fuck out!" "Shut the fuck up!" or "Wake the fuck up!" I probably should have. Looking back at the fact that I was suppressing my instincts for them makes it clear that it was my own fault the place fell apart. There is no such thing as faking it in business. Either things are, or they aren't. I was disobeying the food chain by giving my friends the chance to be equal. We were not equal and did not suffer the same consequences equally either. The same way I would treat other hustlers outside of my business to earn their respect, was the way I should have been treating my friends in business. My friends taught me the importance of putting my foot down in all aspects of my life. If I was going to put it down with friends, it would be double the effect with people I don't know. By not putting my foot down, I helped organize my own arrest. I knew it was coming and did nothing to stop it. Looking in my rear view I now know that screaming on these friends of mine daily would have been the best thing for all of us.

My friends/employees weren't doing their jobs, and it was my job to make sure that they were. You have to draw lines in the sand around what you will and won't do. Speak up and be clear! Don't be afraid to argue for what you know is best. Letting it build into an explosion is not healthy. Let it out by being vocal and stand by what you say. Let there be no mistake on what your opinion is of what's going on. This is a part of earning the respect that people will not simply give to you, but is ultimately required to succeed in business.

Lesson Three:
The Second Chance At Destruction

When you don't trust your gut or put your foot down, you are dishing out second chances. The problem is that you are giving people multiple chances at destroying you. All it takes is one successful attempt from your adversary or even one substantial slip up from a partner and you could meet your demise. So why give out extra chances? Why not be more guarded with opportunities to destroy you? It might sound extreme, but that's exactly what they are. Allowing people a chance to make a mistake is not the same as helping them to take you down. I learned from going to jail twice in three days, and having police contact three times in one week, that these chances I was giving away were career ending. From that week on, I was extremely protective of this aspect of business. After certain mistakes were made by others, I would cut ties with them in terms of business, and learned not to think twice about it.

If offering second, third, and fourth chances is the way you do business, you should call it something else. Business adds up to profitability. This type of behavior adds up to a loss in most situations. In the case that it doesn't, luck has intervened and changed fate for you. Relying on luck is the most irrational way to conduct business of any kind. It won't be necessary if you trust your gut, put your foot down, and stop giving out multiple chances. Then you will be doing business, and the people around you will be the ones relying on luck, hoping you don't fire them.

You Can't Soar Like An Eagle When You're Flying With Turkeys!

You can't soar like an eagle when you're flying with turkeys! That phrase was told to me over twenty years ago, and feels like it grows more true every day. Staying sucker free is a full time job when running a business. It doesn't matter who you are, or what type of business you are running, they're coming. Suckers will show up and set up. It's what they do. You have to be vigilant of their actions to make sure you don't absorb them. Being too close to suckers is close enough to have their ways and habits rub off on you. You might find yourself relaxed with them and telling your connect the same sucker shit they told you. It rubs off and you will eventually receive the same outcomes the suckers around you are attracting.

It doesn't matter what your profession is, suckers exist there too. One of the personalities mentioned in this chapter is present in all environments except for the ones that are designed to drive them out. Keep your professional life professional. The pros don't make simple mistakes and give others chances at blundering opportunities for them. I'm sure if Michael Jordan chose to pass the ball and not take the game winning shot, even his teammates would ask why he would do such a thing. The choices you make for your business can affect it negatively or positively depending on whether or not you are making the right choices.

When it comes to suckers, merely being seen with them can negatively brand your business. It says that you do not make wise choices. You take the kinds of people others don't take serious, seriously. The fact that you know better does not change the perception in the eyes of the beholder. They don't see a bunch of misfits and you. What they see is simply a bunch of misfits. Making a distinction between them and you is not their job. That takes work and effort that is not required of them.

In the end, all of your wasted time and efforts will leave you with no one to blame but yourself. You can't blame a liar for lying, and you can't blame a fuck up for fucking up. The blame lies on the person who watches it and allows it. The responsible person is always responsible for the actions of those around them. People will waste no time asking you why you allowed these things to happen. They won't even look in the sucker's direction. Their focus will be right where it should be, on you. I was taught hanging around four rich people would make you the fifth, and I've learned that hanging around four suckers will also make you the fifth. The choice is yours!

Chapter Eight:
X Factors:
Whatever Can Happen, Will!

Within any business there lies what should be referred to as X-Factors. They represent the unknown variables that make up life's unpredictable nature. No matter what your plan is, and how neatly it is designed, the bottom line is things are "gonna" happen. While there are many things in business that can be prepared for, there is another section of business that requires the ability to respond. These variables are what I would like to discuss in this chapter. Now I certainly can't explain the unknown events that you will face in the future. If I could I would be buying lottery tickets instead of compiling the contents of this book for you. What I will be doing is giving you the gift of shared experience by walking you through some reoccurring X-Factors that I have learned how to manage, and that will be of great benefit to you without having to go through the physical course. This book would not be complete without the X-Factors, so without further adieu, let us open the X-Files.

1. Droughts:

The Drought:
When The Well Runs Dry

What is a drought? A drought by definition is a prolonged absence of something specified. Well to be specific, it's the absence of whatever it is that your selling. A drought can be seasonal or completely unexpected, but it can be a devastating time for your business. Although a drought is only a period of time, you are not guaranteed to survive this period. Some business owners simply can't weather the storm and come out on the other side. One of the most painful things in business to do is turn away a customer. Not only is it counter productive, but it leaves behind a feeling of inadequacy. The drought can create longer periods of being unable to satisfy your customer. It can vary from not being able to obtain your fastest selling product, to being temporarily out of business due to a lack of product, but you can't sell what you don't have.

When in a drought the first thing to do is make adjustments at first glance. This is not the same as panicking. Making adjustments is assessing your business environment and making necessary changes to fit the circumstance. It may mean not taking your wife out to dinner until the price of a particular product comes down. You can't operate in the same manner in a changing environment. You have to be able to adapt to circumstances to overcome them. Having money is the easiest way to adapt to any circumstance. In times of drought, trust is replaced with cold, hard, cash. Make sure you build a reserve to correctly function in times of crisis. You will find that the drought brings out the cream of the crop. This is who is capable of surviving it, because in this situation, business becomes slimmer, making the choice of who to do business with a much more critical one. Take notes from the real life application of these principles below.

Real Life Application: Drought Time

One summer in a studio I had built in Philadelphia, the city was plagued with the biggest weed drought the city has ever seen. We have experienced seasonal droughts many times before that only lasted a month or so. This particular time was a hellish period for the entire city. The lack of weed put the entire city on edge. Without the sale of this beloved herb, smokers couldn't smoke, dealers couldn't deal, and the city's underground economy was turned upside down. Even clothing stores could feel the weed's lack of presence in the streets. In the height of this drought it had gotten to the point that a local radio DJ reached out over the airwaves asking if anyone could find him something and bring it to the radio station. This was a bold move that solidified this drought as one of the most prominent ones in history.

From the inside, the first stage is always the stage of disbelief. It is rooted with the element of rumor. We heard rumblings of it inside the inner circles of the industry, that soon became reality. The attitudes around the city quickly shifted. You could see the demeanor of those around you beginning to change. Some people were able to sustain themselves longer than others, but we were all hungry. Being amongst the connected, we were able to maintain product, but only for those who could pay first. Excuses run high in these times of crisis. At one point the younger brother of a very prominent, multi platinum selling rapper came by our studio with a set of rims to sell. The funny thing is that he didn't want money in exchange for his expensive rims. He was only looking for weed to sell, which in this time was easily considered worth more than money. Nobody purchased his rims that day but he did stay and smoke with us, and that was a valuable commodity in these times, so much so, that it can't be forgotten.

We saw the prices of our product skyrocket over the summer. What was normally a thousand dollar product was now selling for as much as twenty-two hundred dollars. The only thing we could do was rely on the money that we had saved and try to stay afloat in a starving city. Towards the fall, after a three month summer in the city with minimal weed to smoke or sell, things began opening up. It took a while before things began to fully become normal again by way of consignment. After the initial reappearance, my customers who were used to me consigning them could not help me at this time. I had to find a completely new set of customers to purchase the small quantities I was able to provide. I could no longer toss out pounds, instead I needed people who could purchase ounces and smaller. I grew a small base of clients in the neighborhood that the studio was in. This base helped me survive long enough to rebuild what I had lost.

This wicked time in the city exposed a lot of hustlers who merely had the look of success with no money to back it up when the climate changed. It also exposed some immoral natures of some of the people around us. These realities could not be escaped nor erased. This period in time is still talked about today and remains etched into the minds of those who survived it. It was a memorable experience that helped to shape my existence in this game, and one that I also hope I will never have to experience again.

Lessons from story

Lesson One:
Be Prepared

When dealing with a drought of any kind, this is the most valuable lesson there is. Being prepared for a drought simply means stacking your money. It means that you have to prepare for the climate to change. You have to have a reserve that you can rely on in times like this. They do not warn you before arriving. It is the same principle of putting money away for a rainy day. It's not a smart thing to do, it's the only thing to do. You can't allow yourself to get too comfortable in business without creating the proper safety nets for yourself. This means when a particular resource that sustains your business runs dry, you have the ability to purchase from outside sources. These situations require you to have access to cash. Cash is the way you will be able to keep functioning while other business suffer. Even in the case where you are making minimal profits, you are now able to satisfy your customers when your competitors cannot. This may help you to gain customers while others lose them. When business resumes as normal you might find yourself doing better than before.

Lesson Two:
No Consignment

Consignment is cancelled in the wake of a drought. Trust doesn't rhyme with drought, but doubt does! Times of financial crisis must be treated as such. Landlords and utility companies may be sympathetic to your circumstances but it won't go past there. The bills are due when the bills are due. Trusting your product in the hands of another in this instance is gambling against the odds. Some people believe their job is to bring home the bacon. It doesn't matter to them if the bacon was stolen from you. I've had connects come with me to make a sale in drought times after turning the option of consignment off. Droughts can bring out the dark side of business people. Don't expect for everyone to be the same reliable customer that you've come accustomed to working with. You will find customers who have been pressed against the wall financially and are snarling and foaming at the mouth like a wild animal. You must turn off the faucet of consignment and have your customers step up to the plate to bat correctly! This is trickle down business. If your consignment privileges are being restricted, this should let you know that it is the time to do the same in your own position. Pull the reigns back until the situation changes for the better.

Lesson Three:
Be Resourceful

In a drought, being resourceful is a must! You have to be able to fluctuate the flow of your business by focusing on what you can access, while keeping the searchlight on for what you really need. You may need to shift from retail to wholesale, or vice versa. This doesn't mean that this is how your business will remain. It's simply a matter of weathering the storm. This is the time to focus heavily on pushing the products that you do have. Never try to substitute an inferior product without adjusting the cost. If you've had to change an ingredient or alter a product based on the availability of certain products, the cost should reflect that change. It's your task to keep your business flowing as best as you can at all times.

You may very well need to begin reaching out to others at this time. Be careful not to appear panicky and scare away associates. When reaching out, you should be prepared to do real business. You are now getting ready to possibly make transactions with those that you haven't done business with before, and should exhibit many of the principles explored previously in this book. Being resourceful is a mixture of being prepared and being creative. Stay sharp as you venture out into new waters in this extremely critical time.

2. Broke:

Broke:
Diamonds Need Pressure

Being Broke: There's nothing like the feeling of being broke. Most people who have climbed out of financial disparity will tell you that being broke is what fueled their transition. It creates uncomfortable conditions that force your senses to reach new heights. It can be a very special place for the ambitious to be. This is where many powerful ideas are rooted and nurtured into fruition. Hunger can be a serious motivating factor to getting things done. It makes success an instinct for survival, and that can be a powerful force.

The other side of being broke is a very uninviting place. It is filled with negativity, resentment, and other thoughts that create worse conditions that help to further stifle your growth. It is surrounded by pessimism that spoils opportunities and clouds judgment. Being broke for too long can create a stench around your business' aura that will repel people from doing business with you. Let's take a look at the pros and cons of what is presumably a negative circumstance. What you will learn here will help you to better understand how to do business while being broke, or how to conduct yourself while doing business with someone who is broke.

Pros: Broke

Focused: When someone is broke and serious about changing their position they are equipped with laser focus. The details of their plans can be extremely well crafted for success. Being simply unable to afford a loss can sometimes secure a win. It means that your senses are now involved to provide protection when developing a strategy.

Dedicated: Being broke can also heighten someone's dedication level. People focused on releasing themselves of their financial chains are often ready to work longer and more diligently than those that are in a state of comfort. They are not satisfied with merely getting a task done. They are ready for multiple tasks to help them escape their state of ruin.

Loyal: When someone is broke they become beholden to the source of their income. Without access to cash, they are married to consignment scenarios where freedom must be payed for. They have no option available but to accept what is given to create an escape route for themselves.

Creative: Broke is where the magic happens. It's where games like stickball and tag come from. The absence of materials or the ability to provide them creates not only the opportunity, but the necessity to become creative. In business, doing nothing is unacceptable. You have to be creative enough to remain resourceful enough to sustain your business.

Cons: Too Broke

Too hungry: When you are too hungry the sound of your stomach's growling will become a constant distraction. You are now beyond focus and loyalty. Their focus and loyalty now lies with their own hunger pains. Sensibility becomes a luxury that the overly hungry business person cannot afford.

Uninviting looks: Being broke is not the same thing as being too broke. What people aren't aware of is that being too broke has a stench to it. It scares people away from dealing with you, and rightfully so. Too broke is the realm of being unable to afford proper grooming and attire. This must be addressed first because it is a glaring red flag in the eyes of potential clients or partners. When you are too broke, you have to get back to plain broke before conducting business.

Unable to see clearly: When you are too broke you begin to fall victim to business mirages. Any opportunity begins to look profitable in the eyes of someone who is beyond broke. Their vision has been blurred by their circumstances. Plans and strategies must be meticulously scrutinized when coming from someone who is blindingly broke. Their vision is distorted by the possible positive outcome to a seemingly bleak disposition.

Desperate: Inside the mind of the desperately broke is where poor judgment festers. To be plain, when you are "Fucked up" you will do "Fucked up shit". Desperation is the worst component in any business setting. Desperate people are willing to gamble beyond the confines of their own means. They will gamble what is theirs as well as what is not. All of the unnecessary risks in business become necessary to the desperate. Being desperate is equivalent to having horrible credit. Investors beware!

Real Life Application of Being Broke: Time To Win!

After a weed spot in South Philly was unexpectedly closed, my crew and I were in need of a serious influx of money. The spot had exploded, giving the owners of it a thirst for more. The workers, myself being the top one, were placed in a position of hunger for more. We were all in desperate need of setting up shop again quickly to save the workers who had gone broke, and protect the owners from going broke. We sat together in a huge North Philadelphia apartment and mapped out what was one of the most memorable spots in my career. I was very young and had little money to invest into this operation. The money that I had was barely enough to survive a month without income. I was a worker living check to check from the weed spot. The energy in the room amongst us was an extremely serious one. I watched as my older and more experienced mentors carefully designed a masterpiece.

With a lack of funds being present, no detail was left unaddressed. None of us were in a position to ignore what might be awaiting us if we hadn't prepared. Without the money to shop for the right location we were forced into using the only vacant property that was available to us. In the past I've seen spots put together in a matter of a day or two, but financial constraints called for more drastic measures than the ones used before. My good friend and supplier, called and enlisted a friend of his that was a carpenter to make some necessary alterations to the building. He paid the carpenter and promised him extra compensation after the spot began generating capital. Never had I witnessed such detail into the sculpting of this type of project. It was less for our protection, and more for the protection of the much needed funds that would soon be generated. This was a result of hunger. It provided the focus that so many others lacked due to financial comfort.

I had been prepped during the course of construction that upon the spots completion things were going to turn up drastically. By this time I was ready and willing, but had no idea what I was in for. The day finally arrived when the spot was ready for me. I was driven there by my supplier to show me how the place operated. He told me to hurry into the building and shut the door behind us. Walking into the front door of this house was nothing short of amazing. Just on the other side of the door was a 4X4 square foot box that reached the ceiling. The box, once locked from the inside, had absolutely no access to being open from the other side. It was like opening the front door and walking into a phone booth that could not be seen thru. If this wasn't enough I was then made privy to the stash spot that was also custom built into the structure by a professional carpenter. The building was equipped with a removable window sill that fit in place like a puzzle piece. It made it possible to store product inside the wall without being detected. This was an extra precaution made to ensure a lesser chance of a loss. If the spot was raided, it would then be closed down, but at least the product would remain in the wall for us to retrieve later.

When the packages came in I noticed that each individual bag was stapled shut. It was clear he didn't want anyone squeezing out weed to smoke by pinching several bags. It turns out when coupling the stapled bags with the serious construction, customers felt like they were purchasing from a marijuana factory. All of these additions were courtesy of hearing our stomachs growling and allowing nothing to get in the way of quieting that noise.

This particular spot turned out to have a hell of a run that accelerated our incomes significantly. Some may have seen our endeavor as being more than prepared, but when you need a home run to win the game you keep your eye on the ball!

Lesson from story

Lesson One:
Can't Afford To Lose

This lesson is the only lesson in this story that requires any detail. It focuses on that magical place where there is nowhere left to go but up. When you are broke and can't afford to lose you most likely won't. Everything is scrutinized and sometimes harshly addressed. It is where creativity is born and carried out with efficiency. When losing means losing everything, the stakes have become too high for frivolousness to coexist with the construction of your business. The serious nature of this state of being is what will carry you into the next state of being, success. When broke, the fight becomes more than simply attaining money. It becomes a fight for acquiring stability. This is the stability that all people strive for, yet when in entrepreneurial settings it can only be aggressively captured. Broke people should never be counted out, for they are awake and strategizing while others lay comfortably in bed, sound asleep. It forces them into the essence of what business truly is, making things happen to change your situation for the better.

3. Customers:

The Customer Is Always Wrong:
My Way Or The Highway

The mind of the customer is very simple to me. It's not as complex as people would like to make it out to be. Let me ask you this. Imagine a store left you with the option to take all of the store's contents for twenty dollars, with the only condition being that it would cripple the store and it would have to close in a week. Seven days later there would be an out of business sign on the door! This is why the cliche "The customer is always right" can be a dangerous one within the confines of your business. It means keeping things calm and friendly between customer and owner, because I'm sure it can't possibly mean what it implies. It is an obvious fact that customers are what sustain your business. We're now going to look at a few instances in which they are doing the opposite and helping your business to face an uphill battle.

The Alpha: The alpha customer likes to be the aggressor during transactions. They like to impose discounts and price reductions in hopes that you go along with it. They approach sales from angles, rather than head on, and can be just as dangerous as a swindling businessman. Alpha customers are not shy about doing what's best for them, which is being aggressive at getting the product for the lowest possible price.

The Beta: The beta customer feels the authority of the establishment. They are people who didn't know that asking for discounts was even an option. They are respectful to the business and feel that the business is a more powerful entity than they are. Beta customers are the customers that the common cliche "The customer is always right" would most likely be referring to.

The McDonald's franchise may be one of the worlds most well known and successful brands to exist to date. There are many different aspects we can learn from when looking at such a popular brand. When you can post a sign that states that you've served over ninety-nine billion customers, it's fair to say they know a thing or two about working with customers. Let's look at the McDonald's corporation and find out what type of customer they have acquired over the years, and how their relationship with their customer compares to other businesses.

1. McDonald's customers understand the product. The corporation is clear on what it provides. It doesn't leave room for the customer to stand in line and debate nutritional value at the register. There is no confusion pertaining to what's being sold.
2. The restaurants prices are clear and not subject to debate. Prices are displayed prominently and don't give the impression that haggling will be of any benefit. The place commands respect from its customer while providing what is asked.
3. Extra sauce appears to be a product that is given at the owners discretion. It may be due to the quantity of what you have purchased, or the demeanor of the customer that influences the decision, but the worker will retain the final word of the discussion.
4. There is no more that can be discounted than a few pennies. Anything else would not match up and result in an employee termination. No customer would be worth such severe consequences.

Now let's examine your business in comparison to one that has had over ninety-nine billion customers, and let you decide how you measure up.

1. Do your customers understand your product? Is there any convolution that should be addressed before attempting to reel in a sale?
2. Have your prices been clearly established and prominently displayed to avoid any confusion?
3. Do you have a product that has a flexibility involved with it? Is it a product that the customer can clearly see is handled and distributed at your discretion?
4. Are you upfront about discounts and special privileges? Does your customer have the opportunity to take advantage of you?

Answering these questions and reflecting on them will give your business a new edge. You don't have to be involved in the distribution of hamburgers to learn from a giant such as the McDonald's corporation. It is more about the application of these fundamental principles of the business of customer relations that applies in this conversation.

Real Life Application Of Bad Customers: Scram!

When running a block I had built in South Philly, I noticed several different types of customers. The glue that kept them together in my mind was that they were all wrong. They were only concerned with one thing, making their purchase and moving on. A small minority of them were actually concerned with my well being, and even some of them felt they should be compensated for their concerns. Running my corner required discretion. Customers were encouraged to transfer money into my hand via handshake. I would shake the product into their hands in return. Transactions were handled in this way in case we were being watched or recorded by law enforcement. I began noticing a few customers that would immediately hold the product out after receiving it to inspect it on the spot. I would take this as an insult after successfully sneaking product into their possession. Having them expose the product and leave me on the corner to bare the possible repercussions left behind a bad taste. I would constantly chastise these types of individuals trying to train them to spare us both a trip to the precinct. I would eventually have to refrain from dealing with those who wouldn't comply.

Another type of customer that was an utter nuisance to deal with on the corner was the self absorbed customer. These types would pull up in the evening hours and constantly forget to turn the headlights of their cars off. This might seem trivial to you, but when conducting drug sales on a corner a spotlight isn't a necessity. I can understand the forgetful nature of humans helping them to occasionally make this mistake, but I could also spot those that just didn't care about what happened after they left. This is the same problem that I've encountered with people that pull up to the corner with their music blasting. These people exemplify the selfish nature of customers.

I don't want to give you the impression that all of my dealings with customers were negative, because that would be completely false, but among the demographic of negative customers also existed a group of what I refer to as hagglers. The price was never going to be good enough for them. These people were those that would try to pay lower than the deals I had put in place to appease customers. Never wanting to pay full price would spark debates on the corner that took too long to resolve. With traffic picking up the words "Take it or leave it" became protocol with this portion of my clientele, and if that didn't work I kept the words "Get the fuck outta here" close by also.

Lessons from story

Lesson One:
Customers Can't Have Control

When given control, customers don't mind trying to bend and break the boarders between customer and seller. They actually attempt to remove you as the seller and play both roles, telling you the price that they are going to pay. When customers are given too much freedom, it might become the freedom to destroy your business. Always keep control of your business by not allowing the customers to dictate the process. This comes from having a strong enough process in place to begin with. When customers find ways to slip in they will. This is why products have price tags. They are used to establish control. Try not to have hand written prices and regulations. It is too inviting for hagglers to begin haggling.

You have to love your business enough to keep control of it. Don't allow your customer to decide your fate alone. You have some say in the matter. People like to exalt the customer as if they're not providing a service in which the customer is benefiting from. Remember it's your job to be on top of your business and exalting a customer places them above you in your own establishment.

Lesson Two:
Protect Yourself From Your Customers

You must establish rules for your customers. Don't allow your customers to confuse your rules with being petty. When setting up rules for your business you are doing what is best for maintaining the health of your enterprise. If you acknowledge that these things are what's best for your company, you can't allow your customer to convince you that you are being petty. Your customer will not except any and every type of treatment from you because they have set up parameters of what is acceptable for them. Don't be fooled by someone with parameters trying to tear down yours. This will lead to customers destroying what you have built without remorse.

You must enforce the rules that you set for your business and realize that failure to do so may lead to a negative outcome that only you are responsible for. Remember, your goal is to grow a healthy thriving business and not lose what you are building at the hands of those who couldn't care less. Some customers are more parasite than customer. Their job is to destroy the host and then move on to another. Enforcing rules on these parasites will either transform them into the type of customer you desire, or push them away to destroy another business.

Lesson Three:
Define Your Customers Position

Draw clear lines in the sand between yourself and your customers. You must learn to walk that fine line between polite and stern. If need be, you can't hesitate to fire a customer. Being cordial with insubordinate customers can sometimes lead to them overstepping the lines that you have drawn for your business. You cannot give into them, or you will be erasing the borders of what protects you as an owner. Begging and haggling is not a coupon. It should not result in any sort of discount for that type of customer.

It is an insult to the business owner as well as other paying customers.

Make it clear to your customers that it's your business, and you're going to run it as you see fit. You have to find the best way to do this without offending undeserving customers. Certain customers will bring out a more aggressive nature. It will be your job to decide whether it is justified or not. Trust your instincts to protect your business without running away good customers. You may find good customers disguised as bad and bad disguised as good. You are responsible for detecting who is who, and dealing with them accordingly. Basically, you need to learn how to turn on the "asshole" without turning into one!

4. Loyalty vs Free agent:

Loyalty vs Free Agent:
Respect At All Cost

Loyalty: Loyalty in the game is considered to be the act of being loyal to your connects. It means continuously purchasing from one source and being apart of their ups and downs during the course of your dealings with them.

Pros: The good side of being loyal is when it is reciprocated by the connect. This means that you might receive preferential treatment over others in exchange for your loyalty. Having a solid connect who is just as committed as you are can propel your business to new heights that are worth being loyal to.

Cons: The downside to being loyal is abuse. This abuse can take place on the loyal because the loyal are the only ones around to put up with it. Loyal customers are told to bare with the negative conditions of another business.

They are expected to weather the storms without exploring other options. This can be a dangerous position to be in because it possibly places you on a sinking ship, and that is being loyal to sinking to the bottom.

Free Agent: The free agent in business is loyal to the product, and not to who provides it. They have set a standard for their business that they are loyal to, and this means being loyal to what makes sense for them, which leads to growth.

Pros: The great thing about being a free agent is when your connect is aware of this fact. Working with you will now require the best quality of product possible. It ensures your business will be branded in the way that is desirable to you. Your connect will live with the fact that you have other connects who may be able to satisfy you as well. It won't allow them to relax while knowing that you are blindly returning to them for more business. It can also help to keep costs down from your primary source in an attempt to keep you from straying.

Cons: The downside to being a free agent may be a connect holding out on you for those that are loyal to them. This scenario can at times drive costs up for you. When a connect feels like they will see you today and not tomorrow, it compels them to drive the costs up to satisfy their needs. The free agent must also have access to cash. This is what speaks for them in the absence of loyalty.

Real Life Application of Loyalty: The Loyal Free Agent

When reflecting on my career in the weed game I can remember a time when I could have been consigned anything I asked for from a dealer in the North, West, South, or South West section of Philadelphia. I can vividly recall thinking that if I wanted to I could gather up at least fifty pounds in one day if I chose to, from all sections of the city. Many of the people I grew up with were lucky to secure one connect, and would need to be even luckier to keep them. In the street I had a top notch credit score. This made it possible for me to become both loyal as well as a free agent. I could be loyal to the person who was repeatedly dumping product on me, but in the case their product slowed up or the quality shifted I could show my face at another connect's door and be treated as if I was there just yesterday.

Sometimes loyalty can be infused with stupidity. Connects feel that when their product is moving in a conveyor belt type of fashion all existing conditions should remain the same. When this occurred in my business I found that my connect would try to send me weaker product and expect the same push. In the course of business this will happen, but I chose to access other product until his product returned to its original quality. Our flow was interrupted and my connect realized even more just how valuable I truly was. He then approached me with the right product at a cheaper price to pull my business back in once and for all. He realized the risk of having me work with someone else wasn't one worth taking and made the situation more attractive for me. I was looked at as the loyal free agent, someone who would be loyal to a deserving connect without unnecessary deviation, while also maintaining his free agent status in the streets keeping the connects on their toes.

Friends of mine learned not to take personally where I decided to purchase my product. They knew that wherever I chose, was best for me. If I could satisfy my customers and make more money with a stranger long term, then that's what I was going to do. My friends understood that if they met the same criteria as another, I would gladly choose them over a stranger. A free agent decides where to let their loyalty lie and this is what earns the respect of those that you do business with.

Lessons from story

Lesson One:
Loyalty vs Stupidity

You may be placing your loyalty in the wrong place. This is when loyalty has grown into stupidity. This happens when the loyalty isn't equal by way of product, meaning that the product that you were loyal to isn't loyal to you. This will have you being loyal to someone that is giving you something other that what you actually need, and that is not loyalty. That is stupidity! There is a difference between finding a connect and finding the right connect. Having a supplier to simply give you product is a great thing, but having one that is willing to allow you to grow your business is the best thing you could have. Being loyal in instances that stifle growth will place your business on a treadmill. It will run until you are too fatigued to continue. In the business world this is stupidity. Your efforts should always be in attempting to change your position to that of a higher one. If your connect is not meeting this criteria, you should move on.

It is imperative to discuss the possibility of having a connect that does not meet all of your needs, but is in the process of growing. They may need you to help them maintain a larger connect. This type of situation may be of great benefit to you if you are positioned at entry level at the time of the offer. If positioned higher you may want to decline and look for a more solid connect, or possibly fish out the one your connect needed help with. When doing good business, the choice is yours of who you will work with in the game, once the lines of morality aren't crossed, loyalty lies with what can help you to advance. The rest are the bridges that get you there.

Lesson Two:
Know Your Credit Score

In the street, your credit score is all reputation. When you operate based off of the characteristics of a "Sucker", which we've already explored in chapter seven, you are building a negative credit score that is extremely hard to rebuild in the street. In fact, something that I can honestly say that I have never seen before is a street credit score completely restored. That would mean that the memory banks of those around you were stripped away. It is possible for situations to change, forcing a connect to place trust in a former customer with a bad credit score. This will definitely provide the opportunity to rebuild trust as well as your score. The score amongst your peers and associates is built by your actions, and not always repairable with a major influx of cash. I'm sure it will be helpful and appreciated, but it may not help to advance your credit. When discussing morality you will learn in detail how to keep the high score required to remain comfortable in business.

Lesson Three:
Never Personal

Having friends in your business isn't always a plus. Sometimes it creates convolution in the realm of your business. A personal relationship with someone should not equal loyalty in business. If this person is doing strong business then knowing them personally becomes a plus, but knowing them doesn't make their business practices any stronger. Sometimes they have the "now you can buy it from me" mentality. You have to meet this with a sense of being fair. Be clear in the fact that you don't want to be an abusive customer to them. Explain how you're looking for a connect that you can be extremely demanding of. Don't be afraid to tell friends the truth in business.

This also applies to the friend/customer. You don't want to allow friends to ruin your consignment relationships by allowing friendship to blur the lines of your business. Business is never personal. Anyone who continuously takes it personally is not built for it and may want to reconsider. We have to be on the same page in business. Being friends is just the cherry on top, but is not at all required.

Chapter Nine:
Morality Revisited:
Check Your Moral Compass

Karma
What Goes Around Comes Around

Here we are! It is now time to discuss that infinite size, cosmic boomerang that we all affectionately know as karma. This is the principle that implies that what you put into the universe is what you will receive from it. In other words, "What goes around, comes around". While the word karma stems from a Hindu background and religious principle, it can also be found amongst the universal law of cause and effect. The key word here is law. Laws cannot be broken, rules can. The knowing of this fact can possibly be attributed to my criminal mindset, but remains a matter of fact nonetheless. If you think that your actions don't effect your world and the worlds of others, then you have not accepted the reality of the universe.

In the physical world of business, the principle of cause and effect can present itself in some very simple ways. It can be as simple as the way you treat your customers, coworkers, and associates, and the reputation that attaches itself to your business. In the same regard, the respect that you show to other businesses and owners could play a significant role in the way that your business is perceived by the community. In simpler terms, nobody likes an asshole! While there are some situations that clearly warrant the presence of an asshole, you can't allow that to become the overtone of your business model. This backs people away from you, and backing away from you is backing away from your business. Treating people like dollar signs dehumanizes them and forces a natural reaction to remove themselves from your company's presence. Remember, in order to get their money you have to get their business, so your focus should always be on doing business and not simply getting money.

There are many business owners that feel their customers aren't deserving of being treated fairly. They feel that the service that they are providing is worth more than the people they are providing it to. This mentality can do a great deal of damage to your brands karma. Plenty of businesses generate negative karma reports. These are businesses that are last on everyone's list to be patronized. They often carry products of necessity and profit due to circumstance rather than equal exchange. The owners of these businesses treat their customers like prey, and in doing so run the risk of them feeling like prey in the process.

In a dynamic contrast to the previous scenario we can see the element of good karma and the positive effects of what we put fourth also. Some businesses aim to please and receive great benefit from operating in this fashion. These are businesses that are owned by those seeking to earn a customer, and keep them by valuing their business. Some may have a friendly sales approach, while others might offer extra amenities with their services. These are the types of traits that will help people speak about your business in a positive light, and in some cases this translates into more capital for the establishment. Making your customer feel good can yield positive returns for you. Keep in mind these returns won't always be monetary. It may be as simple as the visible smile they're seen leaving with that compels someone else to come in. Nothing is lost in taking a positive approach to doing business. It should be noted that all business endeavors do not end positively, but approaching them from a positive outlook is always your best bet.

All in all, when it comes to business, at the very least should exist a fair exchange. This is the most anyone should ask for. Everything else is extra value or experience for the customer. Extremely lopsided deals are easy targets for increasing or decreasing your karma points. When deals are lopsided they weigh heavily in favor of one side. This may be the case where you are taking advantage of a customer's needs and abusing a situation for your own gain. Adversely you may be on the other end of a lopsided business deal that is in favor of your customer. These types of deals can become tricky because they require you to walk the thin line between providing a more than satisfactory experience, and or falling into a charitable position in your dealings with customers. Of course, all is fair in love and business and it will be up to you to decide how often you will check your moral compass while on your ventures.

Manners:
Raised By Wolves

If you believe that manners don't exist in the street, you will sadly be mistaken. There aren't very many people who were actually raised by wolves. In fact there are so few that they are the extreme anomaly and behaving like them is of no value. Don't misconstrue poverty with being raised by an animal. Manners exist everywhere and are in every facet of life. If you've convinced yourself that, "Please" and "Thank you" aren't relevant during business exchanges, then you may very well just be an asshole. I don't care if you sell drugs for a living or sell legal products, mind your manners. I can't recall any point in my life that I've seen a "thank you" turned down without any prior differences.

Now I'm sure any adult in their right mind is aware that manners go beyond the verbalization of "please" and "thank you". They are interwoven into the way that we do business altogether. Punctuality is a huge premiss of exhibiting good manners within business. In the absence of being punctual, an apology would then be in order. If presented with the opportunity to forewarn someone, an apology should be attached to that warning as well. Leaving someone waiting, or not communicating properly, are both indications of someone with poor manners. If you think its wise to leave someone waiting for you while simultaneously looking out for police and other adversaries without initiating an apology, you won't last very long in the street. People who behave this way leave imprints on those they do business with that sometimes lead to negative outcomes. This is how business turns into someone being chastised like a child, because this is the way children are taught manners. These principles might seem very basic and trivial, but some people feel that the presence of business overrides the need for decent manners. In my opinion, good manners will take you much further than poor ones ever will.

Stealing:
Trust Is All You Have

Whether you're planning on stealing your way to the top, or just occasionally taking advantage of an opportunity, it is a disgustingly unattractive way of being. The karma associated with theft is always negative. It completely obliterates the trust required to operate in business, and in life. Many of us have experimented in taking what isn't ours in our youth. Hopefully the feelings associated with it has steered you into the truth that stealing is wrong, and leads to nothing but dishonesty. It is a temporary situation that provides temporary relief. What is gained from theft can never be fully respected or admired.

In business theft will get you nowhere. You might think stealing from your customer or associate is the same as capitalizing, but there is a huge difference between the two. Capitalizing can be admitted to, while stealing is always denied. Theft in business can range from not alerting someone that they've overpaid, lying to a partner about a price, or just all out stealing. Even a thief with discretion who won't steal from those that he has business with, will find that when something goes missing they will always be suspect number one. This is the logical assumption for anyone interested in protecting their own interest.

The problem with stealing in business is it reflects on one's selfish attributes, and they can't help to further the business of those associated with them. In the street, sometimes the words "starving" and "hungry" are spoken of too loosely. When someone continues to use words that don't actually apply to their situation, they should be watched intensely. If you are starving I would expect you to steal. This is nothing more than self preservation. If I had no money and was going to die today if I didn't eat, after a few honest attempts to obtain what I needed, I might end up stealing food to make it to another day. The twist is when you have people in business who are often implicating that they are in some way starving, to help them to mentally commit to doing the act of a starving person. When it comes to your dealings, don't except thievery in your business. Remember the thief has enough trouble trying to convince themselves it is ok. Don't let them practice on you!

Selfishness:
Stepping Stone Or Bridge?

Not everyone in business will be along for the whole ride, some turn into stepping stones and bridges. The key to differentiating the two is letting them identify themselves. The karmic response to approaching everyone as a stepping stone is not always a good one. Attempting to build bridges and alliances with those you encounter may garner more of a positive outcome. However, in business some stepping stones are stepped on so quickly that they've been identified in hindsight. One of the worst things you can do in business relationships is treat someone who is on your level and can possibly build a bridge with you, as if they were a mere stepping stone. This creates unnecessary animosity that confounds your work environment.

Selfishness is a delicate issue to attack in business because some aspects of business require it. When building your enterprise you do need to have a "Fuck everybody else" mentality, but you can't allow for that to be the perception of your business. Nobody is interested in helping you take over the world. The reality of the matter is you probably won't take over the world, so you better learn how to function in it. After your selfish ways garner your business a spot on the block, don't be afraid to have a few alliances on the battlefield. These alliances may even sell a product that is similar to yours. Once it's established that neither of you are going anywhere, being cordial is better than having an enemy. In the case of a drought or other business anomalies you will need others that you can reach out to in order to keep your business afloat. Every business needs a team to get things done effectively. Members of your extreme reserve team may even work for your competition. This is the nature of the beast. If you'd rather create stepping stones than bridges, make sure you are truly king of the jungle or else you may starve yourself, or worse become someone else's food!

Charity:
Ruthlessness

When people open businesses the goal is to make money, plain and simple. Business and charity are two very separate scenarios that should not be intertwined. The important thing to understand is the difference between the phrase "should not" and "should never," and how they can apply to your own situations. Just because something should not be done doesn't mean it should never be done. For instance, giving away product should not be done, but if someone is starving do you allow them to starve? Aren't there a few innate principles that we as humans share when it comes to the manner in which we treat each other? If a pregnant woman's water broke outside of your towel store, do you not rush to her aid? I'm sure most people would, just out of a sense of decency alone. These types of random situations require the natural, charitable nature of man. The problem is when the perception of charity is presented without being supported by an actual act.

Business does not require charity. Charity should exist on its own platform and should not be entangled with the operation of a business. If you have a charitable heart you will be better off starting a charity rather than a business. You can't allow for the problems of your customers to play on your heartstrings to the point of shrinking margins. It's much better to be fair to yourself, as well as your customer.

This also extends to other businesses that you have work relationships with. Allowing your margins, as well as your time to be abused transforms you into a giver. Business requires a fair exchange, not one giver and one taker. That is better known as a charity, and that is what you should own if you often find yourself in the giving mood.

SuperVillain, Superhero or Citizen?

Super Villain

So who do you vote for in the movie? Are you a fan of the villain? Are you secretly wishing that the villain wins and crushes the superhero? I personally am not. I think the villains are a lot of the times up to no good, and against progression. Now here's the thing, I can also respect someone who cheers for the villain and shares the opposite perspective, as long as they're just as honest about it as I am. If I hear you cheering for the villain, I can respectfully disagree. Now in the case where you are sitting next to me and pretending to vote for the superhero, the respect is gone, and that means disrespect is not off of the table. In my mind the logic is simple. If there are people who want the hero to win, somewhere there is someone in favor of his counterpart. This doesn't bother me in the way it bothers others. I'm bothered by the villain that uses deception of their villainous nature as a tactic to victimize others.

When it comes to business, the super business villain can be a terror in the face of the unsuspecting citizens and heroes in their path. The villain will interact with his victim in one of two ways. The first will be upfront and straight to the point. The second one will be relying on deception to earn a profit without concern for their victim. Let's look further into the characteristics and functions of a super business villain.

The Upfront Super Business Villain

The many types of people that exist in the street also exist in the legitimate world of business. One of those characters is the person that doesn't mind robbing you. He isn't going to wear a mask. He simply allows his position to overpower you into submission to the will of their business. In the street this person is a known villain. The types of villains may range from the kind that will stick a gun in your face with no mask and empty your pockets, to someone who will relentlessly sell products at prices far above their market value. At the end of the day, a robbery is a robbery. The villain's main concern is getting money, not making or earning, but getting. They sometimes go out of their way to remind you that they are villains who care about their wellbeing and nothing else.

The Deceptive Super Business Villain

On the other hand we have the deceptive villain. This is someone who pretends to be a hero or citizen, and uses deception against those around them. This is the type of person that will steal from you, but won't look you in the face and do it. They wait until people turn their backs to rob them. The reason this bothers me the most is because the time spent waiting on someone to turn around is often spent smiling in their face, placating them while simultaneously waiting to carry out a devious act. These people sometimes try to pass off inferior products and services to increase their margins. This is a form of robbery. The difference is they are smiling with you, rather then pressing the nozzle of a gun on you. They will say or do anything to succeed in their business. Customers are expendable to them. They don't mind misleading them into wasting time or energy. This may include someone who will constantly embellish the quality of something just to get the customer close enough to push it on them. They aren't bothered by lying to get you there, or wasting your time. They are ruthless villains seeking domination!

Villain Summary

If you have a villainous nature, embrace it. Put on your villains hat and wear it proudly. If you don't mind taking advantage of people at weak moments or abusing the naive behaviors of those that surround your business, poke your chest out and brandish your villainous "V". Stop trying to disguise yourself as a good guy. It's disingenuous and can very quickly turn a good guy bad. In the end, the choice will be yours. You have to decide what type of villain you are going to be. What bothers you may not bother others. This is an irrefutable fact of life and business!

Super Hero

The fan of a superhero is someone who can appreciate the rescue of the underdog. Seems harmless, doesn't it? The twist occurs when you fall victim to the illusion of saving everyone. When your favorite superhero swoops down to save someone, does that mean that nobody is being robbed across town? What happens when the superhero is sleeping? Does the crime not persist? The reality is that there is no such thing as saving everyone. If that were the case superhero movies wouldn't have sequels, everyone would be saved in the first one. Your superhero mentality might get you squashed like a mortal in the real world of business.

So you think you can do business and help everybody right? Wrong! That's actually extremely brave of you, especially considering the fact that you don't even possess any super powers. I mean at least superheroes know that they won't feel any pain and can still get up after jumping from a cliff. In fact, what superheroes do shouldn't even be considered an act of bravery. I would stop a train too if I knew I wouldn't be hurt. Playing the superhero role without any super powers will quickly get you abused in the true world of business. People know you won't last and will take from you until there is nothing left. Imagine if you remove your hero's super abilities from the movie. How long would it last then? When it comes to dealing with my enterprises, I won't be jumping in front of anything unless my business is the victim.

On the mean streets of Business City, there are two distinct powerless superheroes that attempt to save all customers and associates from all the bad business experiences the world has to offer. These two types are known as Mr. Charity and Super Pushover. Let's take a closer look at the attributes of each of them to see how they may apply to your business.

Superhero Businessman

Mr. Charity: The problem with Mr. Charity is he actually believes that he should save his customers at his own expense. He listens to the personal problems of those he's in business with and allows them to become a priority of his to fix. He offers discounts to anyone he knows before being asked, and when asked for special treatment, Mr. Charity always delivers. He will compromise his margins at any moment for the appearance of helping everyone. Helping everyone might sound like a noble idea, but without the ability to go from idea to magic wand, it will never come into existence. You will merely be giving away the building blocks of your organization brick by brick without receiving any compensation for them. If you were to end up in need, there will be very little if any of the people you have helped waiting to return the favor. You cannot rely on the morals of others. People will take and take, until there is nothing left to take, and you will exit your stupor with nothing but a story to tell.

Super Pushover: Super Pushover's main problem is in the root of a superhero's nature. It is attached to the fact that a hero's key objective is to save someone. Well, for Super Pushover everything that is asked of him he tries to comply with. He allows the customer, as well as connect to adjust prices without ever facing any opposition. He places himself on the losing end of the stick in most business situations, and is unable to gain momentum while those closest to him benefit from his willingness to sacrifice himself daily for others to succeed.

Superhero Summary

If being a superhero is what drives your being, be a superhero for your business. Jump in front of the attacks thrown at your enterprise. Treat your business like the real Lois Lane that is constantly getting into situations that need saving. Protect your business from adversaries and foes looking to take over or crush your endeavors. The villains of Business City have absolutely no remorse for fallen heroes. They may actually take pleasure in the sight of their demise. If being a superhero is where your heart lies, Charity City will be your best bet. This is where your abilities will shine and you can spread your wings as you fly more freely through the skies.

Super Citizen

I think we all understand what a superhero or super villain is all about, but the addition of the super citizen is a creation of my own. In business you will find this to be the smartest character of all. They are dedicated to their own business and don't have to live up to the expectations set by those that seek the extremes of villains and heroes. A citizen isn't required to function like a charity, or be pushed around either. They are citizens, just like the people they serve and that helps to establish a position of no expectations. That is what you want to achieve in business to establish stability while building your company.

When I speak on having no expectations it's important for me to clarify what is meant for you to take full advantage of this principle. The expectations come from getting too close to the nature of a hero, thus rendering confusion in your business environment. When you do business with a hero, you are aware that you can inject personal situations into the equation for extra leverage to come out on top. This is the perception that a hero will leave you with. It appears that they can take it, their business is impenetrable. The citizen on the other hand has the luxury of approaching each situation in the same fashion, which is either "I can help you" or "I can't". The choice is mine!

The citizen can also access the villain's nature from time to time. It might mean taking advantage of a situation for your business' gain. You may raise your prices due to and event bringing in hoards of tourists from out of town. This would be the perfect time to access the nature of the villain. The great thing about being a super citizen is the fact that one villainous act doesn't make you a villain. It makes you someone who is using the power of discretion, and that is the innate power of the citizen that leads to being stronger than both hero and villain. You must decide when to unlock the "super" in you.

Super Citizen's Super Power: The special ability of the Super Citizen in Business City is the most powerful power to have on the mean streets of this dangerous town. It's the ability to use "whatever works" without committing to a particular style. A super citizen can access a super villain's nature and apply it to an instance, rather than have it define their entire construct. The ability to be "super" temporarily becomes the most powerful attribute in the world of business, because you have the ability to use both villainous and heroic attributes while maintaining the flexibility of having the appearance of a mere citizen. This allows them to save only who needs saving, and also allows access to the villain's arsenal.

Super Citizen Summary

Take note that the ability to use your brain, weigh out decisions, and be honest about it, is an extremely useful power in the world of business. It will become a great asset that will only help you to build assets without compromising them. You won't fall victim to customers that possess their own villainous qualities. You can apply the hero in you to saving and protecting what you have built, rather than focusing on those who aren't interested in building at all. In short, the use of discretion is the use of your brain with access to your heart. Operating in the opposite manner by using your heart with access to your brain, will ultimately lead to a crash and burn.

Real Life Application Of Morality: Everyone Won't Fold!

When speaking about morality, the story doesn't need to be too complex. What we are dealing with is simply a matter of right and wrong. At the age of eighteen, just before opening a spot with some friends that changed my life, I was at that broken stage where things just weren't working for me. I was living with my brother in a house that always had at least seven or eight people in it with nowhere to sleep. It had become more of a hustlers refuge than the living quarters it was designed to be. One day I watched a friend of mine make a series of poor decisions that affected the rest of his life. He wanted to go and visit a girl that he knew, but didn't want to take the bus there. An older friend of ours threw him his keys and told him to take his car and enjoy himself. Looking back, I now know that his being ten years older than us provided him with enough wisdom to know the possible outcomes. I also know that he was bored and loved these types of situations for the excitement they provided. Nevertheless, my friend took his keys, as well as the opportunity to get away for a few hours to breeze out.

While driving to West Philadelphia, his mind had apparently began to drift. His head was clouded with all of the stress in our lives at the time, mixed with the radio blasting in his ears struggling to drown out the frustration swirling around his mind. He approached his girlfriend's street and looked for her car to see if she was home. Looking only for her car, and not the cars he should've been looking for caused him to roll through a stop sign right into the passenger door of another car. I think his heart crumpled simultaneously with the exterior of the car he was running into. He pulled over as the man was getting out of his car cussing up a storm and made a split second decision to deal with this another day. He chose to let my friend know what happened first, and address his now hit and run later, crazy I know.

The ride home must have been a blur that quickly came back into focus when he walked in. Here it comes! This guy wouldn't stop, he was going on and on about a car that he cared nothing about, completely out of boredom. In hindsight, I completely understand the frustration that comes when someone who can't give you a penny ruins something that you own, but on the fifth hour of him harping about it, my friend lost it. He snapped and told him that he was going to pay for it and it was time to shut up about it. Although it was very true, it should have never been said, especially to someone like him who could have bought five more of those cars, and was just bored enough to explode all over that type of comment. He looked at him as if he had just taken the bait that he had left and started on how unbelievably crazy he was. This caused tempers and testosterone levels to peak. He couldn't listen to another word. On top of being broke, he was now in the negative. He stormed out and told him he was coming back with his money.

He traveled through the streets of Philadelphia thinking about all of the long shots he could make happen in a short period of time. Only one idea stood out in his head, taking something. A female friend of his had previously tipped him off about someone that she knew that sold large amounts of weed, and always left it laying around. She wanted him to break in, and take the weed to split with her. This literally had gone in one ear and out the other because these types of things didn't reflect our style. My crew preferred earning money over taking money. I've never been a fan of stealing, it doesn't sit well with me, so I never entertained the thought of breaking in somewhere, and I'm sure my friend didn't either. That idea was completely crazy, until this one desperate evening. He told another friend what he was planning, and he recommended taking someone with some experience. All that was left to find was a driver, and he had the perfect person, someone who was good at stealing and couldn't hustle to save his life. He knew he would be willing without much convincing. In fact, just before he left to do this he had changed his mind and the professional thief that he had enlisted convinced him to continue.

This was an all time low for him. He had left the hustler's sanctuary and was now on a mission with a thief and a drug addict to steal from someone who none of us knew. They got to the house at around midnight and approached the back of the house. There were nails facing them on a board that was covering a back window. This was enough to deter my friend from this entire stupid ass mission, but not his chemically dependent associate who threw a cinder block toward the nails creating a way inside. He said that he was in the building for no more than 30 seconds, that's all it took to realize he was taking from someone just like the hustlers he had left behind at the house, and wanted to abandon this mission and his crew. Look at who he was with. They left with about a half pound of high grade weed which he kept for himself. The driver took a shotgun, and there was some cash available for his third partner in stupidity.

When my friend reached home late in the evening, he shocked the entire room with the half pound of weed. I watched as he attempted to hand it to my friend so he would be able to fix his car. To our surprise he refused it. He told him he wanted nothing to do with the stolen product, not even a smoke. My friend was amazed and told him that he made him go do this for nothing, and that he didn't want to hear about the car any more if he wasn't willing to take the money. He agreed and explained to him that he didn't make him do anything. It was his decision to do what he had done, and that the karma was all his to bare. This was a lesson I could never forget from an O.G. by the name of Eng 101. I never saw him fold on his principles and I carried this with me for the rest of my career. However, I myself did smoke that stolen product, but I'm sure you get the point.

Lessons from story

Lesson One:
Stand On Your Principles

My friend was not going to budge. There was nothing anyone could do to get him to accept what he was being offered. He had made up his mind that he was a man of principle and not going to change for anyone. After all, we were in the street, and there was nothing unfair about what was done. It was all part of the game, but just because your in the game doesn't mean you have to take part in every aspect. You have to have your own individual set of rules and guidelines on how to govern yourself, and then consort with those that act as you do. When you set up laws for yourself, the penalty for breaking them can sometimes be more severe than breaking the rules of others. The universe tends to love to rub in the "I told you so" moments to the point of sickness. Maybe that's its way of doing you a favor, by reminding you that your principles are more than frivolous rules. They are part of your makeup as an individual, and when compromised pieces of yourself are lost in the course.

Don't allow your business to force you to challenge your nature. The road to success can be a rocky one. The habits we pick up along the way should be ones that will help us get further along in our endeavors. Don't allow your stomach to speak louder than your heart. You may find yourself stirring up a world of bad karma, or simply eating a good relationship. When the waters of the ocean get rough and dark, your principles serve as the lighthouse to provide direction for you. You wouldn't ignore this light if you were lost at sea. Don't ignore it when the troubles of business make you feel as if you're lost at sea either. Let your morals guide you safely to shore and always remember, don't let the person you become get YOU in trouble!

Lesson Two:
Maintain Your Integrity

When my friend decided to lower himself and behave outside of his character, he found himself among low level people that he shouldn't have consorted with on any level. If his life had ended that day, it would have ended on a mission with a drug addict and a thief. His desperate conditions weren't enough to risk the shame that would've come had he expired that night. Nothing that was going on in his life at that time should have compromised his integrity to that point. The people that he went with probably won't have to reap the Karma that he will from that scenario. Their integrity was never brought into question because they don't have any. Before you can face the world, you must be able to face the mirror. The decisions you make in business will effect you in other facets of your life. Make sure you are comfortable with your choices because they will still be with you when no one else is around.

Maintaining your integrity at all times is a must. Not only will you be occasionally catching your own reflection along the way, but others will be watching you as well. Do you really want people to see you as someone who lacks principle? Or someone who talks a great game, but will drop their morals at the door for any reason? This can leave a bad taste in the hearts and minds of true businessmen. Only in the word businessman should the business come before the man. You have to be a person first, and a good person has a far better chance at being a good businessperson than a bad one does.

Lesson Three:
You Bare The Blame

When you default on your principles and compromise your integrity, the blame is yours. Sharing this is not possible because the lines that were crossed were hand-crafted by you. You knew the entire process of designing them as well as crossing them. Knowing these lines, you knew when they were being approached and had the opportunity of pulling back. Now of course we are all human, and part of the human experience is decorated with error. Learning from these situations is the wisest option to ensure a minimal occurrence of this. What I've found to be a strong remedy for these scenarios is to take your time. Take the time to reflect on your moves before engaging. It may be an hour or a day, maybe even as little as 30 seconds, just make sure you give things thought. We will be exploring the notion of taking your time more heavily in this books final chapter. It applies here because choosing to, or choosing not to take your time is a personal decision that others cannot carry the blame for. This is the difference between someone telling you "I told you so" and you saying it to yourself. You will find in most cases that blaming others won't get you anything but angry!

Chapter Ten:
Hustlin': If I had Wings I Could Fly

L et's talk hustling! After all, that's what this book is all about, how to hustle. Right? The problem is when you take a one-sided approach, because hustling just doesn't work that way. You have to be able to think on your feet as well as think ahead. You often have to review the contents of your rear view mirror to fully understand your position. Hustling is a balancing act between all that you see and don't see in the world of business. It is essentially the game of chess. You have to think before every movement or suffer the consequences. There will also be attacks that you could not possibly foresee coming, that you will have to respond to as if you were made privy to them prior. Hustling represents a limitless world of possibilities. It is not for those with a weak stomach. It can be like a rollercoaster ride with extreme highs and lows that can make you nauseous in the process. Understanding this will help to prepare you as well as aid you on your journey. What I've learned about business coincides with the law of gravity. What goes up will eventually come down. For those of you whose downfall seems like a plummet, remember, if you hit the ground hard enough you will bounce back. Depending on what you are made of, you may even go higher than before.

The best way to describe hustling would be describing the nature of Bruce Lee. Bruce loved his art form to the point that he developed a spiritual connection with it. This meant that he could feel what was invisible. This is an attribute that business owners must adopt. You have to be connected to your business in ways that are unseen to fully be able to exploit its potential. The manifestation of this connection will be greatness. Just like Bruce Lee, your business will take a few blows, but it is the manner in which we show our resilience that will determine the success we achieve.

Bruce Lee entered the world of Martial arts and discovered a great mistake on behalf of his counterparts. He noticed that the fixed positions of karate had become a hinderance for the fighters. They were not adapting to each individual circumstance, but rather relying on fixed positions that weren't effective against someone who was fluid in nature. He often spoke on being like water, stating that it was the softest thing on the planet, yet able to penetrate a rock. This is the nature of a hustler. We must remain soft and elusive to maneuver thru the unknown, but also be effective when we strike by hitting hard and leaving an imprint. It turns out that Bruce Lee can teach us how to knockout the circumstances that attack our businesses, while being agile enough to survive.

In order to equip you on your journey I've organized a few final tips to help you in your travels. In essence, I will encounter the same issue that Bruce Lee has come face to face with before me. No matter how much we equip you with, the fact is that he can't fight, and I can't hustle for you. It will be a culmination of what you have learned and your ability to perform on the fly. Nevertheless, there was a lot to be learned from such a great fighter that has helped fighters of all genres push themselves to their full potential. With that being said, this book could not end without the following information, but as I've stated time and time again in this book, it will be up to you how you apply it in your own situation.

Store Every Number And Be Useful

We've all heard the saying, "It's not what you know, it's who you know". This is a key element of hustling. You simply never know what you will wind up in the middle of. You could be the connection to the next biggest deal and receive a substantial commission, a lump sum off of the top, or at least a healthy tip. These types of situations only happen for the extremely lucky, or the extremely useful. Since relying on luck isn't a practical approach to anything, it's important we discuss how to remain useful in the world of hustling.

Wouldn't you love it if someone called your phone right now and said, "I'm sending you some business."? How about if someone walks into your establishment and says, "Such and such referred me."? When someone makes connections they are stretching themselves. Of course you have to be careful that you are sending people to reputable businessmen, or at least warn them if you haven't done business with them before. The best way to do this is to store every number. When someone speaks to you about their business, it doesn't matter if you need their services or not, their number should be stored. When hustling, the more people you can access the better it is for you.

Let's suppose you are in the process of buying a new car and the salesman mentions he is going to buy an engagement ring for his girlfriend. While shopping for your car you connect your car salesman with a reputable and friendly jeweler that you have met previously. You're now on your phone telling him how you're sending a good guy there for an engagement ring and encouraging the jeweler to take care of them. If your car salesman is seriously interested in buying a ring, what do you think this will do for your car buying experience? How do you think this jeweler will treat you the next time he sees you? When these situations work out they make all three party's smile. It must be noted that you have to judge the character of the people that you link together because sending someone an asshole is never a wise idea. When you introduce people to one another it is your name and reputation on the line. If you feel skeptical of someone's character, the best thing to do is to speak on it. Allow the person you are connecting them with the advantage of knowing that you are sending them business, and not someone who warrants any special treatment. This gives them the room to be on guard while doing business, and that privilege they will ultimately respect you for.

All in all, you will not be able to connect anyone without the numbers to do so. Store these connections and become useful. You may be in the business of selling sneakers and end up selling a pound of weed today. When hustling, the possibilities are endless. Your contact list should be an ever expanding part of your business that provides you with extra arms to help give your business a much farther reach. It is this reach that will make it easier to grasp your goals.

Lawyer Fees & Bail Money

Tell me, what good is a heap of money rolling in if it all rolls right back out? Well, the answer is very simple. Somebody, or a number of different people are making money from your stupidity, so the good that comes from that situation belongs to them. When in the midst of the hustle, there are a million different ways to spend the money that comes in. There are also a million reasons you should try your best to prevent those situations from occurring. In hustling, every day is not the same and money doesn't come in the same flow forever. The entrepreneur must learn how to stack money. Spending your money while in the process of building will make you an employee of your own creation. Money management is the key to your survival in the game.

When you start from zero, it's easy to find success in small increments of money. However, these increments should progress as you do, from implementing goal management. Many multimillion dollar companies were formed by people who were amazed by their first thousand. When coming from zero, that first thousand dollars is enough to fully understand that you have the ability to make money. It's how you handle your opportunity that will determine whether you survive or not. When you reach your goal of a thousand, it will be your choice to either spend your money or raise your goal to five thousand. When I first reached a goal of five thousand my goals jumped to twenty-five. When I reached twenty-five, it leaped to a hundred. You have to be ambitious in your leaps. Setting goals that are obtainable when you push yourself provides discipline and structure. This is exactly what you will need if you're attempting to stack your money. For many people this is not as easy as it sounds. Who would think, watching your own money pile up could be so hard? You won't be able to fully understand it until you experience it. Reassessing your goals will allow you to decide what you have room for in your life, and what is a distraction from achieving your goals.

In the beginning stages of your business it will be much easier to keep your eye on the prize. In the street, building your money is about more than just growing your personal wealth. It often is about saving your ass! When you are attempting to stack your money you will encounter several unexpected situations that had you not been saving your money, you would have found yourself in Shits Creek using your arm for a paddle. In every business you can expect the unexpected. In the street it's much more specific, have your lawyer and bail money ready. If your in the business of selling drugs, you better have enough stashed to fight the case of the crime that you are committing. Nice cars and jewelry won't get you out of jail, cash will! Unless you plan on liquidating your assets for minimal value, you will need to access cash. Remember, no one wants to bail out someone they've seen living the life of splendor and is unable to bail themselves out. This applies to legal and illegal businesses alike. After all, a bailout is a bailout.

Knowing When To Walk Or Run

This is an important principle to have in your arsenal. Knowing when to walk or run is crucial to surviving in the jungle. When you find yourself having a stare down with a lion, it may not be your best bet to run away. Your chances of outrunning this dangerous animal are slim to none. Learning to take into account the probable outcomes for the decisions we make help to remove the gamble that exists within our businesses. Some situations are better to walk into or walk away from, just as others will be more suitable for running. Learning the differences between the two requires seasoning. A seasoned entrepreneur doesn't run towards every opportunity for several different reasons. I've compiled into list form the differences of walking and running in the realm of business. Let's take a look at these references below to strengthen your business practices.

Running:

1. When you are asking for something that will help you in your business venture you shouldn't appear lethargic. You have to move quickly to receive what you're asking for, as well as move quickly to employ its use. You have

to show others that a quick execution will be of better benefit than walking to your goal.

2. Opportunities that come from people that you know are reputable, you should run to. Reputable meaning that you have previously done business with them and are able to refer to your dealings with them. When you are extended invitations from those whom you can see lavishing what they are extending to you, run!

3. Business has a climate. When things are flowing in your business you should be running. Before the climate changes, you should be running to keep up with the current flow of your business. This is similar to the squirrel that runs profusely to obtain enough nuts for the winter. Make sure you study the climate of your business so that you can adjust how fast you run.

Walking:

1. In business, money leverages situations. When you have more than someone you can become prey. In situations where you have more to offer, you have more to lose and these situations should be walked into to give you more time to asses the situation. This is simply not running into a trap. Deals that consist of substantial amounts of money should never be run into. We can often trap ourselves by believing in what we know is too good to be true. If we had only taken the time to walk we would have had the chance for things to unfold on our way. If you don't have an extra thirty-seconds to think then the deal may not be for you. Don't allow people to confuse procrastinating with assessment. You will be robbing yourself.

2. When you are doing business with people you don't know, you have to take the time to observe their business habits. This cannot happen while running.

You have to slow down to be able to see and understand who you are doing business with. Walking into these situations will keep you from appearing too eager and stripping yourself of the leverage needed to properly negotiate. Don't attempt to run a marathon with someone you don't know without walking through the park with them first!

3. Just as climate can tell you when its time to run, it can also dictate when its time to walk. In times of financial crisis it may appear that you should be exhausting all efforts in climbing out of it. The fact of the matter is financial crisis requires focused actions. In other words, slow down. When the climate changes you can run all you want without having anything to show for it. I've witnessed people in droughts running up and down the street, running to every call, ending up with no product and an empty gas tank, all in the name of running. They were just as broke as everyone else, just moving a lot faster. Running against the wind will make a fool out you, not the wind!

Multitasking

Are you getting more than one thing done at a time? Or are you fooling yourself into thinking that you are getting more than one thing done at a time? Sometimes multitasking is a necessary element of business, and sometimes it leads to confusing yourself. This is how people hide things from themselves, misplace things, or lose them altogether. The multi-tasker is really a glorified scatterbrain. We tend to confuse multitasking with prioritizing when we glorify those personalities. Sometimes the busiest people aren't getting a thing done. Their phones are constantly ringing and they can't seem to sit still, always on the go, headed to the next place. From the outside, it might appear that this is what hustling is all about, but in reality, you cannot do more than one thing at a time. The best hustlers are those who can prioritize the best, and manage their time in ways that organize the chaos of running around into what makes sense and not doing what is no more than a waste of time.

You must command your ship. Delegating responsibility is one way of accomplishing more tasks at once. You have to put competent people in position to handle specific responsibilities. This is the only way to correctly do more than one thing at a time successfully. When you are doing too many things at a time, your attention has been divided by situations that require a serious amount of thought. This type of scenario in the street will ultimately end up with an arrest being made. You have to diligently focus your energy to task. If you're going to be on the block, then be on the block. Don't divide your attention to other things and invite people who are on different journeys into this type of setting. You should be in search of those that can be an extension of yourself to carry out the duties that you cannot physically attend to. This is the importance of chapter six, Sucker Free. This will help you to fully understand the multi-task.

There is such a thing as doing too much. You cannot divide your attention. Your attention should be focused and applied to the tasks at hand. I can remember over ten years ago hiding eighteen pounds of weed from myself in my own home, due to being focused on too many things. We as entrepreneurs have to learn the value of priorities and scheduling to avoid becoming scattered in our operations. Take a time out to reevaluate your life and business, and how they coincide with one another. If you don't take the time to do so, you may find yourself doing a whole lot of nothing, or worse a whole lot of time!

Quitting Time

While growing your business, there is a high probability that you have struggled with the concept of quitting. What you have to remember is that in the world of business your ultimate goal is to achieve success. When in search of success, quitting is never an option, however transformation is. In my lifetime I've used several different vehicles on my road to success, the latest one being this very book. One of my life's goals was to be a success, and my businesses were vehicles that I've used to get there. I grew up selling weed. Does this mean that becoming a marijuana kingpin is the only option for me to obtain success? There can come a point in you business when it stops making sense. Should you fight to keep your business alive? Yes, you should with all the strength you can muster! Should you use that same muster to bring a dead horse back to life? Probably not. This applies to the two types of crazy spoken of in the very beginning of chapter two. You have to remain conscious of when you are entering the realm of the "real" crazy and not the "business" type of crazy.

All in all, there is no specific quitting time. If you are invested in your success, it should only be a period of transformation or reinvention into a new stage of business. Remember, business is a mindset. The businesses we operate are the vehicles we use on the road to success. With that being said, I've had several cars in my life, and look forward to quite a few more. These businesses have helped to shape me into the person that I am, and for that I am grateful for all of those experiences. When you can learn from a failure, you have actually gained something extremely valuable.

Momentum

It's now time for the final words of this manual. I've chosen to end it this way because this is what I wish for all of you, momentum. Momentum is that point in time when what has been aerodynamically crafted has just enough speed, and just enough power to take flight. This is the point where you won't be able to listen to anyone. You are now becoming airborne, and your attention will be diverted to the fact that you are leaving the ground. You simply will not be able to hear the words of the gravity impaired. You won't be aware of the others that are flying high above you while you are taking flight. This is the temporary moment when you are experiencing a business high that you have earned and should be enjoyed, and later celebrated.

After you have taken flight, you will now have to open your ears and eyes again and snap out of that euphoria. You have to be mindful of the advice of those who have been flying before you and take it into account while maneuvering the success of your operation. You will find that different levels of success bring many changes, but the ground rules that got you in the air will always apply. You should also remember that once you've taken flight, the words of those less successful still hold value and are not always void of content. What goes up must come down, but the application of etiquette will be the difference between a smooth landing or a crash. Hopefully you'll be gassing up while in the air! Happy Hustlin'!

Real Life Application of Momentum:

Now it's your turn to fill in the blank!